CRAFTWORK
IN COLOUR

Better Homes

CRAFTWORK IN COLOUR

COLLINS LONDON AND GLASGOW

ISBN 0 00 435516 4

Contents

Creative Machine Stitching

Beautiful handmade items for your home reflect your own interests and taste. They are personal treasures you will cherish and enjoy for years to come. Whether you sew by hand or with a sewing machine, distinctive and useful stitchcraft will give you a sense of real satisfaction.

Using a sewing machine, you can create any of the attractive designs shown: the rocking-chair cover (page 8); the rich pattern of fruit (page 9, foot); on page 10, the bold printed cushions and striped stool cover (left), delicate pink cushions (right) and bedspread (foot) in red, varied with shapes of yellow, orange and purple; and the floral wall hanging (page 11).

Rocking Chair Cover

You can make a traditional rocking chair the centre of interest with a new contemporary cover. The hot pinks, purples, oranges, golds and reds are appliquéd on to a striped background material with rows of stitching running up and down. The stripe in the background material should be placed vertically so that the stitching will lose itself after leaving the appliquéd shapes.

Allowing for turnings, make paper patterns for the back, headrest and seat covers. Pin these to a striped furnishing fabric.

Next, cut the required number of pieces of coloured felt, varying the shapes by having some triangular and some irregular four-sided figures. To these large shapes tack smaller circular shapes, leaf shapes and circles to add interest, and then place the large shapes attractively on the striped background material by using pins placed horizontally to the line the machine stitching will make, so that the machine needle can work over them. Using a normal length of stitch sew vertically over the felt pieces and background material to give a textured effect. With the right sides facing, seam together the three edges of each cushion; turn. Fill the headrest and seat cushion with kapok, and the backrest with a pad of foam rubber. Close the remaining edges carefully, slip-stitching by hand.

Trapunto

For an interesting cushion cover or decoration, the design on a printed fabric can be outlined by stitching as in the pattern of fruit in a basket (below, left), making it stand out from the background by using padding between the print and a backing material. In this variation of trapunto, the stitching holds the top, padding and backing together, creating shapes in relief as each outline is completed. If you wish, baste the three layers together before you start stitching. Soft fabrics are easiest to work with.

Another variation of the technique of trapunto is shown on page 10. The striped fabric on the stool seat (page 10, left) alternates one stuffed line of fabric with one flat. Sew one edge of the striped heavy cotton material to the backing material, which should be a strong canvas, lay cotton cording between the striped material and background, then sew second edge of the stripe completing a raised stripe by so doing.

Space the raised stripes regularly on the fabric; if random stripes are made, then vary stuffed and unstuffed stripes irregularly also. After the lines have been stuffed with cording, edge the cover with a colourful bias binding which matches the fabric and stool, and tack the two side edges of the cover in place to the wooden frame of the stool from underneath.

Cushion Covers

For the printed cotton cushion, leaning against the stool (page 10, left), allow more material than is needed for the design to allow for stuffing. Having placed the material for the design over the backing, machine-sew two-thirds of the distance around each flower; add stuffing between the print and the backing, then complete the shape by stitching. The back of the cushion could be the same material as the front. The cushion can be machined together on the wrong side when the right sides of back and front are placed together. The cover can then be turned to the right side, stuffed with kapok and slip-stitched along its fourth side without removing the fabric from the machine.

To make the red cushion, cut a circular piece of paper a suitable size for the centre motif. Fold this circle in half, then again into quarters and again into eighths. Cut the edge away from the centre into a symmetrical curve while the paper is still folded, then unfold and use as a pattern for the design.

The material for both the motif and the background could be cotton, velvet or satin, and the design applied using a Satin stitch on your machine. The cord motifs could then be added by couching by hand with an invisible thread completing the top of the cushion. Add the back, and stuff in the usual way.

Favourite designs are captured on the pink cushions (page 10, right). For the rectangular one, cut a square piece of linen, cotton, flannel or any other pleasing and durable material, using half for the front and the rest for the back. Pin or baste appliqué pieces to the top using a different colour but a similar material. Stitch with wide solid Zigzag on large pieces, narrower width on small ones.

Quilt

The warm quilt uses rectangles $4\frac{1}{2} \times 8\frac{1}{2}$ inches and $4\frac{1}{2}$ inch squares. Pin these on backing fabric and machine sew with Zigzag or Chain stitch. Finish with hand or machine-sewn stars.

Floral Wall Hanging

Combine the techniques of appliqué and machine stitching to get the effects of a floral decoration as in the wall hanging (above). Anyone who can sew a straight seam can draw penlike lines to hold the appliqué in place. Use scraps of felt, denim and linen collected from previous sewing efforts. The thread used is the same as you use for regular sewing.

For the background, use a piece of off-white nubbly woollen material. Cut out a leaf-shape in green felt; tack it to the background. Cut flowers and small leaves out of felt and hessian; tack these to the large leaf.

Remove the presser foot from your sewing machine and attach the darning foot; put feeder teeth out of action and if possible set the machine to low. A zigzag or fully automatic machine should be set to free action. Use a needle suitable for medium-to-heavy weight fabric; and test upper and lower tension to make sure the stitch is even and correct for the fabric.

Starting at the outer edge, machine-stitch each flower, following the design. Work slowly and steadily. Continue from flower to flower without cutting the thread, varying the pattern the stitching makes in each shape to add further interest, and ending with the stems.

If the material tends to pucker as the embroidery progresses, stitch the design on an embroidery frame. These frames are sold in most shops dealing with embroidery threads or sewing machines and are intended to keep the material taut while it is being machined. Most sewing machine and craft shops have leaflets and books on machine embroidery.

Rugs

Rug-making is a most satisfying craft giving scope for design ability and a most useful end-product to grace your home.

Abstract or geometric designs are really the most suitable for rug-making, but the first consideration must always be the character of the room in which the finished rug will be placed. Obviously an abstract or geometric design will be wrong for a chintzy room or on a floral carpet. Here a compromise must be made and highly conventionalized floral motifs and leaves used.

Felt Rugs

Felt is an ideal material to use for rug-making. No turnings have to be allowed as felt edges do not fray, however intricate the motifs in the design. The grain of the material can be completely forgotten too, as felt has no warp or weft and so shapes may be sewn to the background at any angle without the danger of puckering, as would be the case with woven materials. Great care must be taken, however, with the preliminary

tacking as the success of the rug depends on each applied shape lying flat on the background. Each shape should be tacked outwards from the centre, first a vertical line from the centre to the top of the shape, then to complete the vertical from the centre down to the lower edge of the shape; again from the centre, at right angles to the vertical, a horizontal line to the right hand edge; back to the centre again and the horizontal completed outwards to the left hand edge of the shape. Parallel lines of tacking should be made to both the first horizontal and the first vertical line until the applied shape lies completely flat on the background ready for its outer edge to be sewn to the background with a decorative stitch either by machine or by hand.

Anyone who can thread a needle can make a felt rug, for the hearth, or just to brighten a floor. Three examples of the sort of patterns which can be invented are the rich maroon and purple rug (page 12) and the gay green and gold design (page 13, foot). The wall hanging (page 13, right) uses the same pattern and the same technique, while the nursery rug (below, right) has simple animal and letter shapes.

Felt rugs are not only easy to make, but fairly inexpensive too. Vivid colour combinations can be used, to match or contrast with other furnishings in the room. A heavy weight felt is preferable for the base colour, with the design pieces appliquéd directly to the background.

Tack the pieces carefully into place first of all, then set the machine for full-width Satin stitch and use a heavy weight thread as near as possible in colour to the felt. For hand-sewing, use a Satin stitch or Buttonhole stitch (see pages 47–8). Trim with cotton or wool fringing, making sure that it overlaps the raw edges.

Vary the width, length and character of strips sewn to a solid felt base as shown in the maroon and purple rug (page 12). Several arrangements of these toning colours can be tried out and the final arrangement pinned and basted before being sewn. To avoid wrinkling always sew in the same direction. To finish off, top-stitch fringing to the rug edge.

Felt motifs in shades of gold, white, light and dark green with contrasting touches of mandarin orange and red are combined in the design for a wall hanging or a rug (page 13). Parts of the design could also be used for a screen, or a placemat.

A rubber rug pad or carpet pad can be used to make a rug skidproof or, alternatively, you can paint the underside with liquid designed for this purpose. Spray the finished rug with dirt-resistant liquid. These rugs should always be dry-cleaned.

For hooked rugs (above and page 15) see instructions pages 16–17.

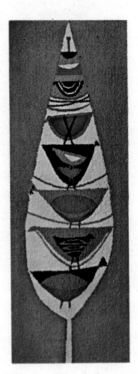

Hooked Rugs

Making rugs is a beautiful craft and a rugging hook obtainable at any haberdashery counter can be used to make any of the attractive rugs on pages 14–17, or, by the same method, the wall hanging with the blue background (above). Cushion covers or stool seats could also be made in this way. Knotting with this kind of hook is a challenge to your imagination, whether you use a kit with a made-up design or set about making up your own patterns and colour schemes.

Choose sharp, pure colours to work these designs. Similar kits (available in various sizes) make hardwearing rugs suitable for any room.

Rug-making kits include all the materials required: $\frac{1}{4}$ inch mesh canvas with the design stamped on, a rugging hook and wool already cut into short lengths.

Method

The method is very straightforward. Working on the right side of the canvas, the hook is put through the canvas to the wrong side, where a piece of pre-cut wool is held in the left hand under the canvas, with cut ends of the wool together so that a loop is formed. The hook catches the loop and pulls it through to the right side. Then, with the loop still on the hook, the hook is pushed back to the wrong side of the canvas through the next space in the mesh, where it catches the two cut ends of wool and pulls them back through the canvas and then through the loop to the right side. The ends are then pulled tightly to form a knot and the tufts left on the right side.

The height of the tufts can be varied by cutting them to different lengths on the right side. When knotting cushion covers, low tufts are best, whereas for wall hangings and rugs medium height tufts are best, and the highest can be used to achieve a three-dimensional effect. The spacing of the loops is regulated automatically by the background canvas.

The bold rug (page 14, left) which has an oriental look, provides colour in a light hallway; a clear red background emerges as a perfect foil to the intricate black and blue pattern.

The hearthside rug (page 15) in rich tones of yellow, bronze, gold and white on a deep olive background, goes beautifully in front of a blazing fire. Choose a background shade which will blend with the other furnishings.

Rich colours, blue, bronze, mustard, green and red are interwoven lavishly on a white background in the bedside rug (page 16, left). A design of this kind could be used in either a bedroom or sitting-room.

A rug hook lets you paint with rug wool as an artist does with oils. The wall hanging (page 16, right) in rich blues, greens and olive accentuated in black and white is one example. Make it by exactly the same technique as that described for rugs, on page 16.

For a different style of design, perhaps for an entrance hall, at the bottom of a stairway, or beside a bed, you might like to try to work your own double eagle rug (page 17, top). In this

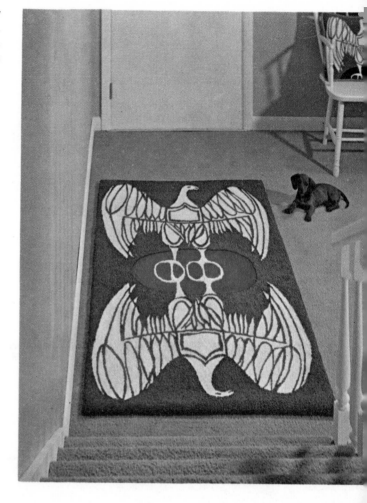

example the use of strong colour emphasizes the bold design.

A contemporary rug such as this, in blues and reds (page 17, foot), is amazingly quick to make using the same rug hook. To get a clear pattern on the right side of the piece you are working on, it is best to use contrasting colours side by side so that there is no possibility of colours merging into one another and spoiling the bold effect.

Less involved designs than on these rugs will give beginners a chance to experiment with the hook before attempting a rug or wall hanging. A kit for a footstool cover would be a good starting point, and this can be bought from any craft or needlework shop. Hooking can easily be done by holding the work on your knees; a frame is not required. However, some people do prefer to use one.

One step which applies to all these items is to allow more canvas than necessary for the size of article you are making. Turn the surplus to the back and stick it down firmly with latex adhesive. Then cover the whole underside with non-slip backing (obtainable from hardware shops).

Appliqué for a Bedroom

All the charming designs described in this section are produced by means of appliqué: the crown and diamond patterned quilt (above) the headboard with its stylized flowers (page 19); and on pages 22–5, bed linen and towels edged with geometric birds or, for a child's room, scampering rabbits.

Full instructions and patterns for the quilt are given on pages 19–21; instructions for the headboard are given below and for the bird and rabbit designs, on pages 22–5.

Appliqué is an extremely effective technique and not difficult to do, but one detail of the method must be very carefully observed and always borne in mind. When planning the shapes to be applied to the background, the way of the material must be considered very carefully before the shapes are cut out. That is, the warp and weft of the cut shapes must match the warp and weft of the background when they are placed at the angle at which they are to be sewn. If this point is neglected a twist or pucker may occur in spite of careful tacking.

type silhouettes out of paper, varying the shape and size but keeping in scale with the size of the headboard. Add the stems and arrange in a satisfying pattern on the background. Using these shapes as patterns cut out pieces in materials of varied colour and texture, and sew on to the background with a full width Satin stitch, adding extra touches such as stamens, or veins on leaves and stems by hand.

Mount the finished embroidery by stretching it over a piece of hardboard to fit a frame the size required for the finished headboard. Free-form designs with simple outlines which make use of a variety of textures are most effective for this type of appliqué work. For example, try blending coarse fabrics with waffle weave and velveteens.

Flowery Headboard

Choose a smooth-textured fabric such as linen or heavy cotton for the headboard (below). Start the design by cutting simple flower type and leaf

Crown Quilt

Crowns and diamonds decorate the quilt illustrated on page 18. To make the pattern fit different bed sizes, simply add or subtract lines of the motif. The attractiveness of the design can be enhanced by varying textures and fabrics so as to complement

your bedroom furnishings. The dramatic motif is easy to sew by machine, and once you have mastered the basic crown and diamond pattern you will find it an attractive design for long or short curtains too.

Linen would be an ideal material for the crown quilt. The sharp angles of the motifs would be more manageable and fray less than a heavier material. You will need six pieces of light turquoise blue, six of an olive green, six of yellow, six of black, and six of white, as shown in the diagram on page 20. The different coloured pieces are given letters for easy reference. Of course you can use your own combination of colours.

Materials

1. Cotton bedspread: plain colour, single or double. If you are making the bedspread yourself, use a close-textured cotton or linen; 9½ yards of 36 inch for 4 foot 6 inch bed, 6½ for 3 foot.
2. For the appliqué: 3 yards of satin finish cotton in assorted colours. Each design unit is of two pieces of different colours appliquéd to the background. If you are using six colours, you will need ½ yard of each colour.
3. Thread to match both the bedspread and the appliqué colours.

To Make Bedspread

1. Double bed size: cut 36 inch wide material into three lengths of 113 inches each. Cut one of the lengths 22 inches wide. With a half inch seam, baste the three lengths together, side by side, with the narrower 22 inch width in the centre.
2. Twin bed size: cut two lengths 113 inches × 36 inches wide. With ½ inch seam baste these two lengths together.
3. Sew seams on both double bed size and on single bed size by machine, or by hand using back-stitch.
4. Fold the bedspread in half lengthwise and cut a gentle curve on the lower outer corners, making sure in this way that both corners are the same. This makes a neat corner for draping on the bed.
5. By machine, or by hand, using back-stitch, make a ½ inch hem all around.

To Make Appliqué

1. Using 1 inch squared paper (rather than tissue) make several crown patterns.
2. Pin the patterns on to the fabrics and cut. You will need 36 pieces. There are 18 design units, and each unit is made of two pieces of harmonizing or contrasting colours.
3. Place the bedspread on a flat surface. From

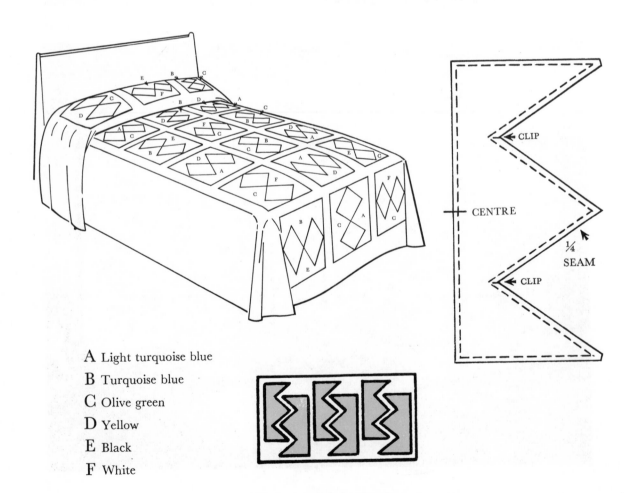

A Light turquoise blue
B Turquoise blue
C Olive green
D Yellow
E Black
F White

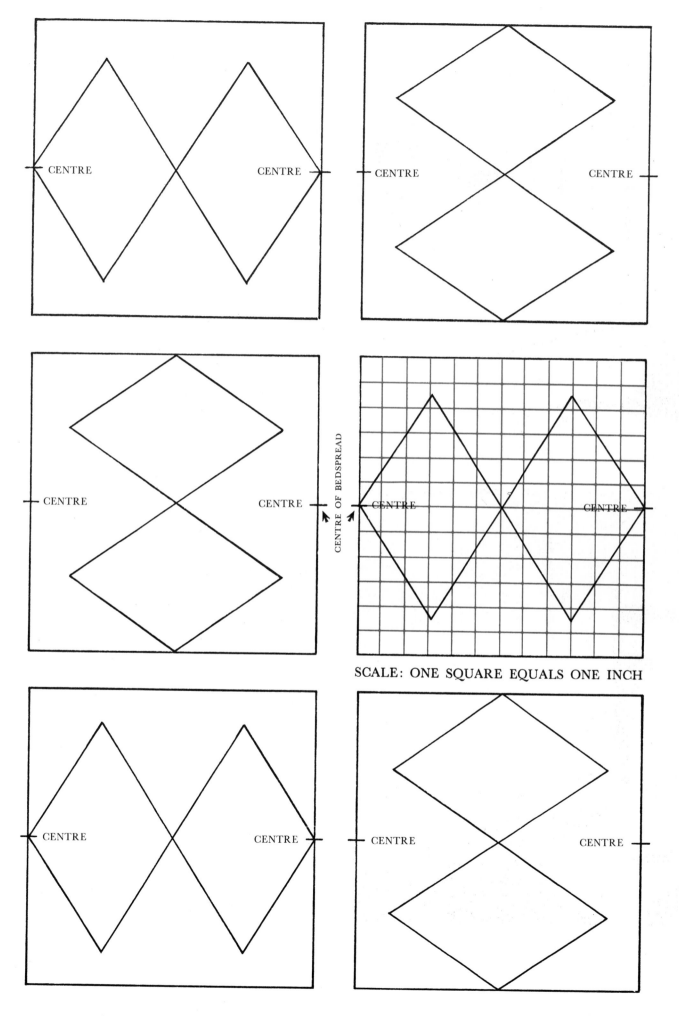

SCALE: ONE SQUARE EQUALS ONE INCH

the top centre of the bedspread measure down 5½ inches. Mark this spot by inserting a pin.

4. Place two pieces of the appliqué horizontally, with centre points meeting at the spot you have just marked. Turn under ¾ inch edge, pin, and baste in place, with the points of the crowns meeting.

5. 3½ inches to the right of this appliqué, line up two more pieces of appliqué; this time vertically, with points meeting. Turn under ¾ inch. Pin and baste.

6. Repeat step 5, but to the left of the centre appliqué design.

7. Directly from the bottom of each of these appliqué designs, measure down 13 inches and mark with pins. This allows a space for the tuck-in under the pillow.

8. Place three more design units at these markings in line with the top three appliqués, alternating horizontal and vertical as before. Each design unit in this row is 3½ inches apart. (If the bedspread is made as directed above, the seams can be used as the guides for lining up the appliqué design, the inner edges of two outside design units being placed on the seams.)

9. From the bottom of the row of appliqués, measure down 2¼ inches and repeat step 8.

10. Continue from step 9 until there are six rows in all (including top row above pillow turn-under) with three design units in each row.

11. Machine-stitch the design to the bedspread, with Straight stitch, Satin stitch cording or Herringbone stitch.

Bed Linen

With a minimum of time and effort you can apply clever designs to any plain coloured sheets and towels. Only the simplest kind of Satin stitch is needed for these designs. Geometric birds (top left) are perched facing right and left in co-ordinated colours. Directions and patterns are given below and opposite.

Scampering bunnies (below, left), make a playful addition to brighten a child's room. Details of the design are given on pages 23–5.

BIRD DESIGN

Patterns for the five bird designs needed are given on page 23. The designs are shown appliquéd on to a pillowcase, sheet, facecloth and two towels. For appliqué choose contrasting colours in any soft fabric, such as cotton. Place iron-on interfacing under the appliqué fabric for machine-sewing. Use mercerized thread matching the colours of the appliqués.

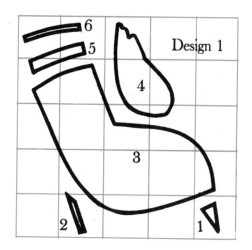

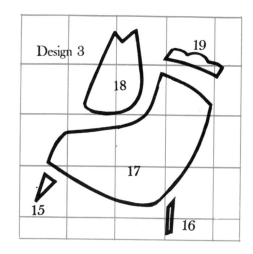

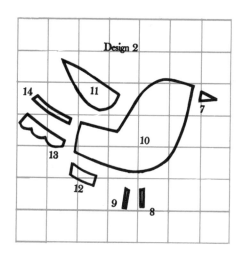

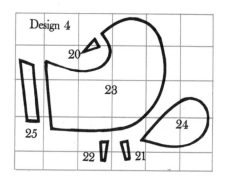

Pillowcase

1. Expand the designs (this page) to required size for patterns. Each square represents one inch. For a pillowcase, you will need one of each of the five designs (one set). When placed on the pillowcase, each design is centred along the hem area.

2. The bird designs face both right and left; cut each as the pattern indicates. When cutting, place the appliqué patterns on the right side of the fabric.

3. Apply iron-on interfacing to the wrong side of fabric to be appliquéd. The added stiffening will make machine-sewing easier.

4. Place the patterns on the appliqué fabric. Draw around patterns. The appliqué pieces are numbered and must be applied numerically to the fabric; watch the illustration carefully for correct positioning.

5. Cut out the appliqué pieces, following the drawn lines, and keeping each of the design units together.

6. Pin each piece of one design unit on to the

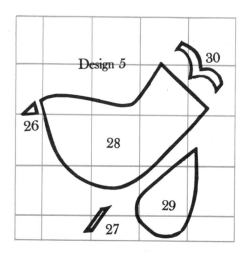

pillowcase following numerical order. Complete the first design before proceeding to the other designs.

7. With thread matching each appliqué piece, machine-stitch, using a Satin stitch, around each piece. A single line of stitching may be used for the birds' legs if you wish.

Sheet

When the sheet is appliquéd, the designs will cover the entire width of the sheet, with patterns centred along the top hem area. For the left side of the sheet you will need designs 1, 2, 3, 4, 5, 2, 3, 4. They will be put on to the left side in that order. For the right side you will need designs 5, 4, 3, 2, 1, 5, 4, 3, also in that order. Repeat steps 2 and 3, as for the pillowcase. Cut out the patterns; cut the required number of designs to cover the entire width of the sheet. Keep design units together.

Repeat steps 5, 6 and 7 to finish the sheet.

Bath towel

For the bath towel you will need four designs, 1, 4, 3 and 5. They should be put on the bath towel edge in that order. Repeat steps 2 and 3 as for pillowcase. Cut out the appliqué patterns for the four designs, keeping each design unit together for easy working.

Repeat steps 5, 6 and 7 to finish the towel.

Hand towel

For the hand towel use two or three designs depending on width. The method is the same as for the bath towel.

Facecloth

For the facecloth you will need only design 1. This design is put just above any decorative border on the cloth. Repeat steps 2 and 3 as for pillowcase.

Cut out the appliqué pattern for the design, keeping the unit together.

Repeat steps 5, 6 and 7 to finish the facecloth.

RABBIT DESIGN

This design is used to appliqué a pillowcase, sheet, bath towel, hand towel and facecloth. For the appliqué fabric, choose a soft material in a contrasting colour. Have on hand iron-on interfacing (which will be used under the appliqué) and thread matching the fabric to be appliquéd.

Pillowcase

1. Trace the designs full size to make paper patterns. For the pillowcase, you will need B, C, F, A, E and F, to be put on the pillowcase in that order. Each design is centred along the hem line of the pillowcase.

2. When tracing the patterns, notice that the rabbits face both right and left. Trace as the patterns indicate. (When cutting out the designs from the appliqué fabric, make sure that you place the patterns on the right side of the fabric.)

3. Apply iron-on interfacing to the wrong side of appliqué fabric (the added stiffening makes machining easier).

4. Now place the traced patterns, which are already cut out, on the appliqué material reinforced with interfacing and draw around the patterns.

5. Cut out the traced appliqué pieces, following the drawn lines and marking right and wrong sides clearly (with tailor's chalk, for example).

6. Pin each piece on to the pillowcase following the order given above.

7. Machine-stitch (using Satin stitch) each appliqué piece to the pillowcase. Then press the appliqués with a warm iron.

Sheet

The design runs across the width of the sheet; the patterns are placed right way up along the top hem of the sheet. In the centre of the sheet use design piece A. For the left half, use design pieces C, D, A, E, F, C, F, E in that order; for the right half, use design pieces B, C, A, B, C, E, D, C, in that order. Repeat steps 2, 3 and 4 given above for the pillowcase. Cut out patterns and then cut out the required number of designs. To finish off the sheet, repeat steps 6 and 7 as for the pillowcase.

Bath towel

You will need designs A, E, D and C, in that order, applied above the border of the towel. Repeat steps 2, 3 and 4 as for pillowcase. Cut out the patterns required and then repeat steps 6 and 7 to finish off the bath towel.

Hand towel

You will need designs A, D and B. Apply in that order above the border. Repeat steps 2, 3 and 4 as for pillowcase. Cut out the appliqué, and repeat steps 6 and 7.

Facecloth

You will need design E only. Apply just above the border or across the corner. Repeat steps 2 and 3 as for pillowcase. Cut out the appliqué and then repeat steps 6 and 7.

DESIGN   A

DESIGN   B

DESIGN   C

DESIGN   D

DESIGN   E

DESIGN   F

ACTUAL SIZE

Quilting

Simple colour schemes and designs are the secret of the eye-catching bedspread (below), the seat for a hanging cane chair (page 27, top) and the screen (page 27, foot). The essentials to know before you can begin quilting are the area you wish to cover and the amount of material this will require.

All these examples of quilting are done with a Stab stitch to outline each piece and the method used is known as English or Durham quilting.

Bedspread

For the bedspread, first of all decide on the width of strips you wish to use and the number of colours. Then measure the bed to be covered and allow for the size of overhang you wish.

The bedspread illustrated measures $5\frac{1}{2} \times 7\frac{1}{2}$ feet and the quilting takes 7 yards of heavy cotton rep. This should be divided amongst the six or so colours you expect to use, so that the shade to be emphasized predominates.

Make sure that all the strips are the same width (the finished width is about $1\frac{1}{8}$ inches and the seam allowance should be $\frac{1}{4}$ inch on each

side). To eliminate waste divide the strips evenly into the fabric widths. Cut the pieces in lengths varying from 4 to 12 inches and, selecting colours and lengths at random, start to machine-stitch the ends of the pieces together (avoiding two lengths the same colour next to each other), first in twos, then in fours, and next into long strips the desired width of the bedspread. When you have a quantity of these, choose two, see that the colours where they are joined fall in different places, and seam them together, keeping the stitching smooth and the narrow joining seam flat. Continue sewing the strips together until the quilt is the desired length. Another method you might find less cumbersome is to make the top in several crosswise sections and so reduce the weight of material in the machine. When enough sections are completed to make up the desired length of the quilt, sew them together and so complete the top before machine-stitching them together. Press all the crosswise seams open. Now you can begin the quilting.

Use a heavy cotton rep again for the backing. You will need two widths of material to harmonize with the colours of the quilt top. Sew these together and press the centre seam open. Use a flannel blanket, or cotton or Terylene as filling. Spread the backing, wrong side up, on the floor; centre the filling over it. Spread the quilt top right side up, over the filling, allowing at least $1\frac{1}{2}$ inches of backing to extend all round.

Beginning at the centre of the quilt, pin (placing pins at 6 inch intervals) or baste the

three layers together, working toward the outside. Tack first along the vertical axis and then through the horizontal axis. Continue pinning or basting in parallel lines on either side of each axis until the quilt is completed.

Use a colour of thread which harmonizes with all the colours in the quilt top (single or double thread, as you prefer), begin quilting at the centre, working out in all directions. Each block of the top is quilted by hand with small even stitches about $\frac{1}{8}$ inch inside the seams.

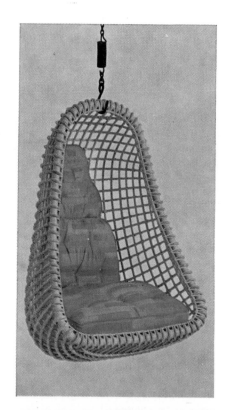

When sewing on a quilting frame (which is not absolutely necessary) make tiny stitches, each one in two movements: the first straight down through the fabric to the other side; and the next straight back up. Generally, the space between stitches as seen from the top should be somewhat longer than the length of the stitch itself.

If working without a quilting frame, it is best to pass the needle in and out of the fabric in a single movement. This allows the fabric to hump upwards a bit where the needle is under it and the stitch is sure to go completely through all layers. Make only one stitch at a time to produce the slightly rippled effect which is characteristic of quilting.

When the entire top has been quilted, run a straight line of machining around the quilt edge, then trim evenly. Finish the edge with bias binding (about $1\frac{1}{2}$ inches wide) in the same colour as the backing. This will make a border about $\frac{1}{2}$ inch wide. However, if enough backing has been left all round, then this can be folded and whipped down to make a $\frac{1}{2}$ inch finished hem for the border.

Cane Chair Cushions

A paper pattern must first be made to fit the seat and back of the chair. Using the same technique as for the bedspread, cut gay strips of hessian to fit this pattern when they are sewn together. Measure carefully round the edge of the pattern and construct a welt to the desired thickness of the cushion. Using the paper pattern again, cut the back of the cushion in hessian to contrast in colour with one of the colours used on the front of the cushion. Mark the centre front of the top of the cushion and the centre front top and bottom of the welt. Pin centre of top to centre top of welt and back the top to welt on the wrong side. Mark the centre front of the back of the cushion and pin to centre bottom of welt. Tack welt to back of cushion leaving an opening for stuffing with kapok. Machine on tacked lines, turn to right side, stuff and top-stitch the opening.

Screen

The screen is covered with quilted panels kept in place by large brass upholstery tacks.

Patchwork

Patchwork is a form of needlework in which pieces of cloth are sewn together to make an article. The origins of the craft are lost but primitive forms existed before handwriting and probably grew out of the necessity to patch and mend garments. All types of fabric have been used, linens, prints, silks, velvets, partly worn clothes and even leather.

There are two ways of making patchwork. One is to stitch the patches to a background fabric, rather like appliqué. The other is to stitch the patches together and build up a whole fabric; this is true patchwork. Many articles may be made using this method but traditionally it was used for quilts, bedspreads, curtains, cushions, rugs and upholstery.

Materials are often chosen in order to produce the modern, bold, geometric designs used today. Plain cottons or linens in contrasting colours, or tones of one colour can be very effective, but the colours need to be carefully balanced in the overall design such as the outlines on pages 29 and 30. Black, white and grey are effectively used in the design on page 31.

In the old method of using up scraps and partly worn clothing, care should be taken that one type of fabric only is used in each article, that is, cottons and linens together or silks and satins together. In using this method an effort should be made to balance plain and printed pieces and colours to give a pleasing effect.

The designs are worked out with a basic template shape or possibly two templates, as in Figures 3 and 8.

The traditional shapes normally used in the 18th and 19th centuries were the scale shown in Figures 4 and 5 and the hexagon shown in Figures 1, 2 and 3. Both these shapes are based on the circle, and for a hexagon the radius is marked off six times round the circumference of the circle to obtain the shape. Figures 1 and 4 show how they may be drawn with ruler and compasses. It is essential to be accurate when drawing and cutting out the templates, as the shapes, when joined together, must make a flat, whole, fabric. Use the designs illustrated on pages 28–30, or for new ideas for designs, study pictures of tiling and mosaics or use the rectangular shapes in parquet flooring.

The template should be carefully cut out of stiff card, or better still, thin perspex. Something hard-wearing is advisable as it will have to be drawn round many times. Using thick brown or white paper and the template, cut quite a number of exactly similar shapes. These paper shapes are then pinned to the wrong side of the fabric and cut, allowing a $\frac{1}{4}$ inch turning all round. With the paper template still pinned to the fabric, turn the $\frac{1}{4}$ inch turning back over the edge of the paper and tack through the paper fabric, taking care to fold neatly at any corners.

When several of these have been made they may be joined together. Take two of the pieces to be joined, hold them right sides together with right sides matching, paper side out, and overcast the edges together with fine needle and thread, taking care that the needle does not go through the paper.

A more modern technique would be to cut shapes in iron-on interfacing, using the template. The interfacing need not be discarded and would give more body to the finished article.

Continue in this way until one shape is surrounded by others, when it might be convenient to unpick the tacking and remove the paper. The whole article is built up in this way and when final tackings and paper are removed it is carefully pressed on the wrong side.

All patchwork is lined to cover the seams with one of the materials used for the patchwork. It may also be interlined by placing wadding between patchwork and lining, and quilted along the seams. Alternatively the seams could be effectively decorated with a Herring-bone or Feather stitch in a neutral colour.

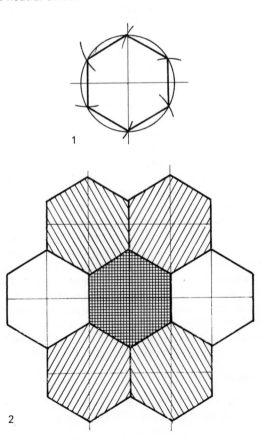

1

2

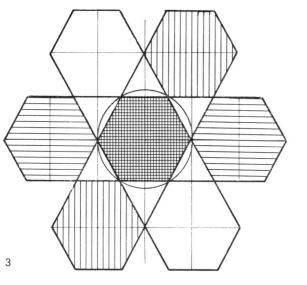

3

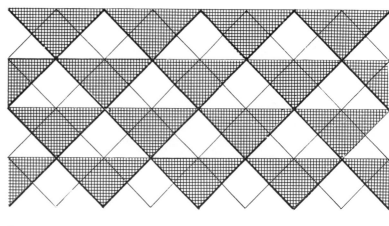

7

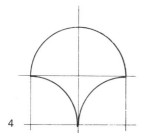

4

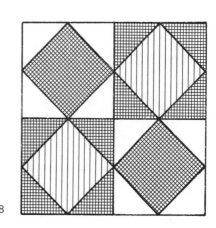

8

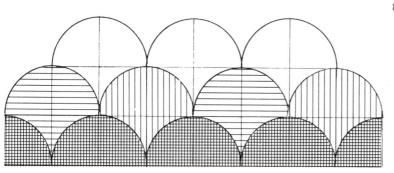

5

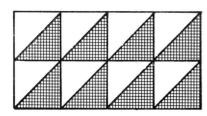

6

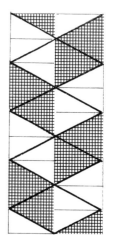

9

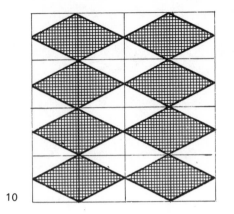

10

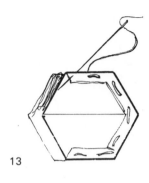

13

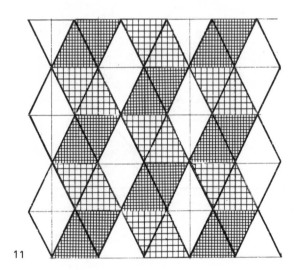

11

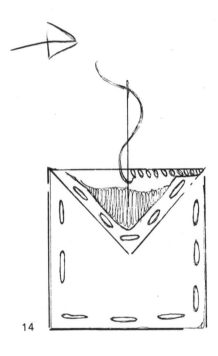

14

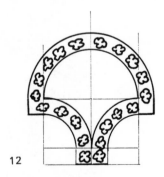

12

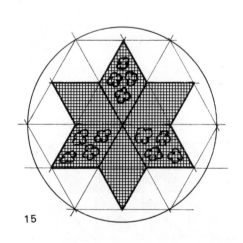

15

A more decorative and less solid effect may be achieved by joining the shapes with open seams. The edges of the shapes could be blanket-stitched and whipped together, or a row of double crochet worked into the Blanket stitch before whipping them together. This method requires fairly large shapes, otherwise it is difficult to carry out.

Patchwork
Sewing Box Lid

This attractive design makes use of plain, checked and patterned cotton in colours of grey, white and black. The diamond shape of the template has sharp angles giving interest to the related colours used.

Knitting

In the past, creative knitting for the home was limited by the lack of variety in wools. Now there is such a choice of exciting materials including nylon and Courtelle that there is little excuse for *not* knitting. All you need to know are the basic stitches; all you need to buy is wool, needles, and a pattern.

Matching chair cushions and placemats (above) bring a dining area up to date. The tie-on cushions are knitted in turquoise, amethyst, blue and black; but the colour scheme can be changed to match any room, and the size can be altered to fit other chairs.

The hanging light fitting has a slip-on cover made of linen yarn. The three cushion covers (page 32, foot) can be knitted in colours that will brighten up a room. They are quick to make in standard 4-ply wool and an effective way of freshening up old cushions. Finally, try the soft fluffy Afghan rug (page 34) which can be draped on a chair or sofa. Here it is shown in a blend of coral mohair and rust-coloured wool which knits up quickly. Complete instructions for all these attractive designs are given on the following pages.

If you are feeling really ambitious you can cover an armchair using approximately the same techniques. Make paper patterns to cover the seat, arms and back of your favourite armchair. Using a hard-wearing, pre-shrunk wool and a firm stitch, such as Moss stitch, knit shapes to fit the patterns, allowing extra length on the inside of the back of the chair and on the sides of the seat and insides of the arms to allow for a 'tuck in'. Assemble the shapes by pinning them together (using the chair as a dummy), machine twice on the pinned line, turn to the right side and pull on over the chair.

Moss stitch is done by knitting one plain, one purl row alternatively with one purl, one plain row.

ABBREVIATIONS (for patterns on pages 33–7)
k: knit; p: purl; st(s): stitch(es); sl: slip; tog: together; psso: pass slipped stitch over; rnd: round; dp: double-pointed needle; wo: wool over; rem: remaining; m: knitting two stitches into one; wo reversed: wrap wool backward over needle twice; rep: repeat.
( ) Repeat instructions within ( ) as many times as specified outside ( ).
Repeat whatever follows as many times as specified.

Chair Seat Covers (page 32, top)

Materials

Foam rubber to make the cushion, approx. 1 yard ⅝ inch thick; 3 oz. 4-ply wool in three colours (e.g. 1 oz. each amethyst, deep blue and turquoise); 8 oz. 4-ply wool in a fourth colour (e.g. black); 5 balls mercerized crochet cotton (e.g. 1 oz. each deep blue, purple and bright blue; 2 oz. black). No. 6 knitting needles.

Tension. 4½ sts to 1 inch when pressed. Plan carefully the number of stitches needed to fit the chair seat.

Instructions

Front. With black cotton and wool together cast on the appropriate number of stitches. K 1 row. P 1 row. Rep 3 times. K 3 sts in black (k 6 sts in blue, sl 2 black) rep ( ) ending with 6 blue, add black and k 3. P 3 black (p 6 blue, sl 2 black) rep ( ). P 3 black. Rep the above 2 rows 3 times.

With black only, k 1 row, p 1 row. K 3 black, change to turquoise k2 (sl 2 black, k6) repeat ( ) k 2 turquoise, k 3 black. P across keeping pattern and colour. Rep above 2 rows 3 times. With black only, k 1 row, p 1 row.

Amethyst row is same as blue row. There are 13 colour rows ending in blue.

With black only, k 1 row, p 1 row. In order to shape the back of the cushion, at the beginning of next 2 rows cast off 10 sts. At the beginning of next 2 rows cast off 15 sts, cast off remaining sts.

Press the cover well and finish with a row of single crochet across the top to make the curved shape more even.

Back. With mercerized crochet cotton and wool, cast on the same number of stitches as for front, k 1 row, p 1 row, until the back is the same size as the front. Shape the top the same way and press the whole back.

Ties. Single crochet with wool and cotton together to make four 9 inch ties for each cushion. Stitch these in place and use to secure the cushion to the chair.

Placemat (page 32, top)

Finished size 13 inches × 19 inches.
Materials
4 spools of (10/2) linen handweaving wool (e.g. blue), No. 7 knitting needles.
Tension 4 sts to 1 inch when pressed.
Instructions
With two strands of linen cast on 53 sts loosely. K 1 row, p 1 row, rep this 8 times for border. K 3 sts * wo, k 2 tog* rep across, k last 2 sts. P across row. Rep these 2 rows 5 times. K 1 row, p 1 row. K 3 sts, * wo k 2 tog* rep across, k last 2 sts. P across row. Rep these 2 rows 5 times. K 1 row, p 1 row, rep 2 times. K 3 sts, * wo, k 2 tog* rep across, k last 2 sts. P across row. Rep these 2 rows 5 times. K 1 row, p 1 row, k 1 row, p 1 row. K 3 sts, *wo, k 2 tog* repeat across, k last 2 sts. P across row. Rep these 2 rows 5 times. K 1 row, p 1 row. K 3 sts, * wo, k 2 tog* rep across, k last 2 sts. P across row. Rep these two rows 5 times. K 1 row, p 1 row, 8 times, cast off.

Green Cushion (page 32, left)

Finished size 14 inches × 14 inches.
Materials
5 oz. 4-ply wool (e.g. green); 2 balls mercerized crochet cotton. No. 7 knitting needles or size to obtain correct guage. Marker.
Tension. 4 sts to 1 inch when pressed.
Instructions
Front. Cast on 53 sts with cotton and wool, k 1 row, p 1 row. *1st row:* k 2, put on marker. This is the beginning of every odd row. The pattern directions start after the marker. K 1 *wo, sl 1,

k 1, psso, k 7, k 2 tog, wo, k 1* repeat * to *, put on marker, (k 2 end of odd row). *2nd row:* all even rows are p. *3rd row:* k 1* wo, k 1, sl 1, k 1, psso, m 5, k 2 tog, k 1 wo, k 1* repeat* to* k 2. *5th row:* k 1 wo, k 2, sl 1, k 1, psso, k 3, k 2 tog, k 2, wo, k 1 *repeat* to* k 2. *7th row:* k 1 *wo, k 3, sl 1, k 1, psso, k 1, k 2 tog, k 3, wo, k 1* repeat * to * k 2. *9th row:* k 1 *wo, k 4, sl 1, k 2 tog, psso, k 4, wo, k 1* repeat * to * k 2. *11th row:* k 1 * k 3, k 2 tog wo, k 1, wo, sl 1, k 1, psso, k 4* repeat * to * k 2. *13th row:* k 1 * k 2, k 2 tog, k 1, wo, k 1, wo, k 1, psso, k 3* repeat * to * k 2. *15th row:* k 1 * k 1, k 2 tog, k 2, wo, k 1, wo, k 3, sl 1, k 1, psso, k 2* repeat * to * k 2. *17th row:* k 1 * k 2 tog, k 3, wo, k 1, wo, k 3, sl 1, k 1, psso * k 1 * repeat * to * k 2. *19th row:* k 2 tog * k 4, wo, k 1, wo, k 4, sl 1, k 2 tog, psso * repeat * to * ending k 4, sl 1, k 1, psso k 2.

Repeat the above pattern four times ending with a p row and then cast off.

Back. Cast on 56 sts., k 1 row, p 1 row. Continue until the back is the same size as the front.

Pressing. Press front and back to 14½ inches.

Lining. Make the lining of cotton to match the crochet cotton colour.

Putting together. Use a single crochet stitch working with the pattern of the cushion towards you.

Turquoise Cushion (page 32, right)

Finished size 11 inches × 11 inches with 1½ inch welt.
Materials

4 oz. 4-ply wool (e.g. peacock blue); 4 balls twisted embroidery thread. No. 7 knitting needles or size to obtain correct gauge. Marker.

Tension. 4 sts to 1 inch when pressed.
Instructions

Front. Cast on 46 sts with cotton and wool, k 1 row, p 1 row. *1st row:* k 2, put on marker. P 2 * keep wool in front and sl 1 wool to the back and k 2 tog, psso, wo 2 reversed to make 2 sts on needle. P 2 * marker, k 2. *2nd row:* p 2, k 2 * p 1, k 1, into over, p 1, k 2, * repeat * to *, marker ending in p 2. *3rd row:* k 2 * p 2, k 3* repeat * to * ending in p 2, k 2. *4th row:* p 2, k 2, *p 3, k 2, * repeat * to *, ending in p 2. Repeat the 4 pattern rows 12 times; do the first 2 rows of the pattern. K 1 row, p 1 row, cast off.

Back. Cast on 42 sts, k 1 row, p 1 row, repeat until piece is the same size as the front. The cushion can be made completely reversible.

Pressing. Press front and back pieces to 11¼ inches.

Side piece. Cast on 6 sts, k 1 row, p 1 row for 10¾ inches, k 3 rows, * (repeat three times to make four sides); cast off. Press 1½ inches wide and each section 11½ inches long.

Inside lining. Make a covering for the cushion of any plain cotton material that matches the thread.

Putting together. Single crochet the front piece to the side piece, making sure that the ridge is at the corners. Single crochet the back piece to the sides, leaving enough room to slip in the cushion before finishing.

Striped cushion (page 32, middle)

Finished size 13 inches × 19 inches.
Materials

2 oz. 4-ply wool in two colours (e.g. 1 oz. each emerald green and turquoise); 4 oz. 4-ply wool in a third colour (e.g. navy blue); 4 balls mercerized crochet cotton (e.g. one each green, turquoise, and two of black). No. 7 knitting needles.

Tension. 4 sts to 1 inch when pressed.
Instructions (working right to left as shown in the illustration).

Front. Cast on 50 sts with black cotton and blue wool. K 1 row, p 1 row loosely. *1st row:* k 1, put on marker, p 2 * wo, sl 2, p 2, pass the 2 slipped stitches over * repeat * to * ending p 2, k 1. *2nd row:* p 1, k 2, * k 1 (k 1, p 1, k 1) into over * repeat * to * ending in k 2, p 1. *3rd row:* k. (Knit this row loosely.) Repeat above three rows three times, p 1 row. Change to green wool and turquoise cotton and repeat above pattern. Change to blue wool and black cotton and repeat above pattern. Change to turquoise wool and green cotton and repeat above pattern. Change to blue wool and black cotton and repeat above pattern. Change to green wool and turquoise cotton and repeat above pattern. Change to blue wool and black cotton and repeat above pattern. Change to turquoise wool and green cotton and repeat above pattern. P 1 row. Cast off on knit row.

Back. Cast on 50 sts with black cotton and blue wool. K 1 row, p 1 row until the back of the cushion is the same size as the front.

Pressing. Press front and back to 13½ inches × 19½ inches.

Inside lining. Make a covering for the cushion using cotton (e.g. blue) for the back. For the front make a striped cover using colours contrasting with the knitted stripes (e.g. green cotton behind the turquoise stripes).

Putting together. Use a single crochet stitch while holding the front of the cushion towards you. Work with the black cotton and the blue wool.

Afghan rug

Finished size 48 inches × 65 inches.
Materials

Sixteen 1 oz. balls mohair (e.g. coral); four 4 oz. skeins Twist knitting wool (e.g. rust). No. 11

35

knitting needles 29 inches round or size for correct gauge. 1 large crochet hook.

The rug is knitted 65 inches wide and 48 inches long, instead of knitting 48 inches wide and 65 inches long. The rib is widthways instead of lengthways.

Tension approximately 2½ sts to 1 inch.

Instructions

Cast on loosely 176 sts on a rnd needle 29 inches long, size 11. Using Twist wool k 1 row, p 1 row. Change to mohair. *1st row:* (preparation row only) *wo, sl 1 (purl), k 1 * repeat. *2nd row:* *wo, sl 1 (purl), k 2 tog * repeat. *3rd and 4th rows:* same as 2nd row. Change to Twist wool and repeat 2nd row, four times. Repeat the above until 13 balls of mohair are used (save the other 3 for the fringe). K 1 row, p 1 row with Twist wool and cast off. To make a firm edge for the fringe, loosely pick up 176 sts with Twist wool and cast off. Do this at the beginning and end of rug. At the other two edges, pick up sts with Twist wool, 4 sts for every 8 rows of pattern (2 sts in the mohair row, 2 sts in the Twist wool row). K 1 row, p 1 row 3 times. K 3 rows, p 1 row, k 1 row, p 1 row, k 1 row, p 1 row, k 1 row, p 1 row, cast off. Turn back and hem.

Fringe

A most attractive finish to the rug is achieved by adding a 6 inch long fringe to each side. Each knot of the fringe is made from three 12 inch strands of mohair plus one 12 inch strand of Twist wool.

To make sure all the strands for the fringe are the same length, cut a template from stiff card 12 inches long and 2 or 3 inches wide. Wind the mohair lengthwise round the template, then tie firmly through the groups of loops of wool at the top and bottom of the card. Slip the loops off the card and cut through all the loops at each tie. Repeat this operation with the Twist wool until there are sufficient strands of both mohair and Twist wool to complete the fringe.

Take three strands of mohair and one strand of Twist wool and, with eight ends matching, fold in half to make a loop 6 inches long. Put the crochet hook through the corner of the right side of the rug, two rows up from the cast off edge, pull the loop through to the right side and thread the eight ends through the loop in a bunch. Pull tightly into a knot. Repeat this 88 times along both sides of the rug. Alternatively, a neater fringe might be achieved by cutting a template in firm card 6 inches long. Wind the mohair lengthwise round the template, then tie firmly through the loops of wool at the top and bottom of the card. Slip the loops off the card, put the crochet hook through the corner edge of the rug and replace one of the ties by the hook. Pull this loop through to the right side and replace the hook with the thumb and finger and pull the other tie through this loop. Pull tightly to form a knot. Repeat 88 times along the side of the rug.

Ready made fringes are obtainable in the larger drapers' shops and these could be hand-sewn to the rug taking great care not to stretch the edge in the process.

A fringe of bobbles would make another attractive finish to the rug. Make them by cutting a series of circles in stiff card. The circles should be the desired circumference of the finished bobbles with a hole punched in the centre of each. Put two of these circles together and cover them with very close stitches by taking the thread through the centre and over the edge of the circle and back again through the centre continuously. When the whole circumference of the card is covered, slip the scissors in between the two circles of card and cut all the threads at the outside edge, draw a thread through between the two cards, and wind it several times very tightly round the threads. Fasten it off with a knot and leave the ends long enough to form a little cord by means of which the ball may afterwards be tied to the rug; this done, make a snip in the cards, pull them out and the bobble is finished.

Knitting on a Loom

Knitting on a loom is the best way to tackle heavy woollen articles like the green fringed shawl (page 37, right) or the striped scarf (page 37, foot). Admittedly, it is rather slower than ordinary knitting, but it keeps the weight on the table; and it is a stimulating change for anyone who wants to try something different.

Attractive designs could be attempted if a longer loom were made with wider spacing between nails. Various gay colours of rug wool used to make a striped design should give a very striking result.

The loom shown in the sketch (page 37) measures 3¾ inches × 27½ inches, and is 4¼ inches high. These measurements can, of course, be adjusted to suit individual needs. For this loom,

46 wire nails were set in two parallel rows of 23 as shown in the diagram, with $\frac{1}{2}$ inch space between each nail and $\frac{1}{2}$ inch space between each row. The nails stood about $\frac{1}{2}$ inch above the surface of the loom.

To thread the loom, follow one of the two methods shown in diagrams A and B (this page). Knot the wool to the first nail, then run the wool over every alternate nail in one direction, then back over the empty nails. Repeat, so that there are two threads around each nail.

To start knitting, pick up the lower thread with a crochet hook, pull the loop over the thread above and drop it on the other side of the nail. Continue until the row has been completed.

Now set up the threading pattern again, but this time adding only one row of wool by running the wool over every alternate nail in one direction, then back over the empty nails. Knit up the bottom threads as before.

Continue in this way until the article is the length required. To finish off: beginning at the right hand side of the loom, pick up the end stitch of one row and drop it over the corresponding nail on the opposite row. Take the lower thread on this nail and knit it over the top one in the same way. Continue in this manner to the end of the row.

Return to the right hand side, take the loop off the first nail and drop it over the second nail; then knit the lower stitch over the upper. Continue in this way to the end of the row, and last stitch. Cut a short length of wool from the free end and draw it through the remaining stitch. Darn in the end.

Materials needed to make a knitting loom

Two lengths of hardwood 27$\frac{1}{2}$ inches long, 2 inches wide and 1 inch thick; 2 smaller pieces of hardwood 4$\frac{1}{4}$ inches long, 3$\frac{1}{4}$ inches wide and 1 inch thick; 8 flat-headed wood screws, 1 inch long; 46 No. 16 wire brads.

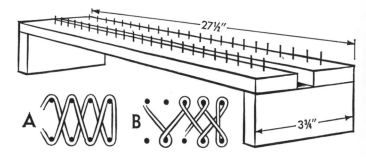

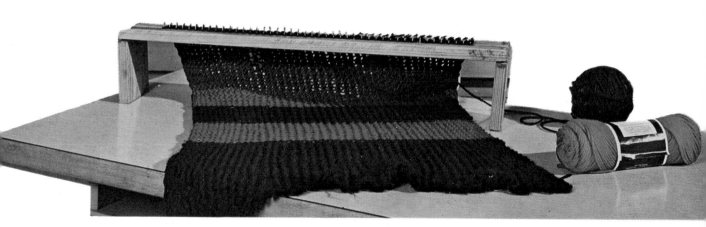

Crocheting

1

2

3

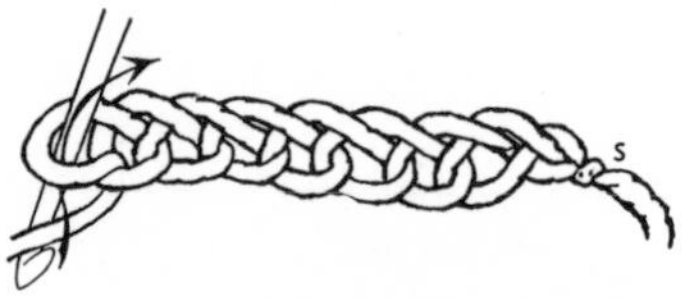

4

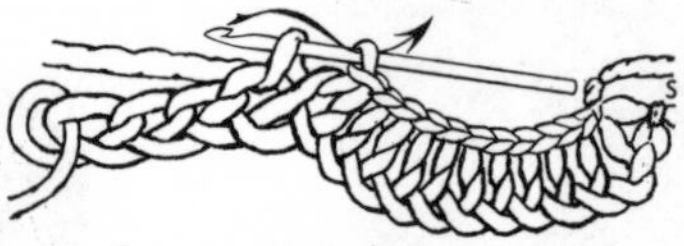

5

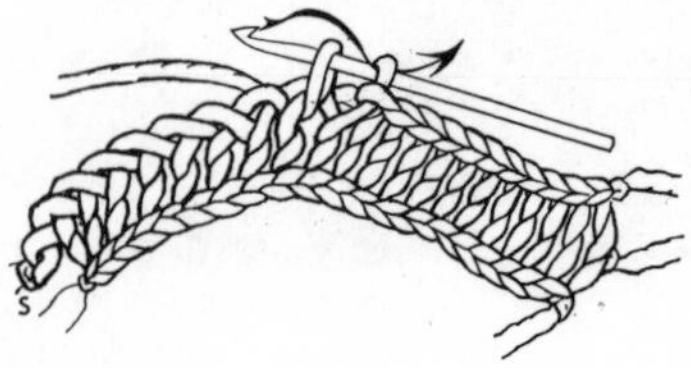

6

Crocheting is a very old art. The beginner need not be concerned with the difficulties involved in the art of crochet; they are virtually non-existent. No equipment is needed beyond crochet hooks of various sizes and a variety of threads. The hooks may be metal, bone, wood or plastic and are numbered according to size; the lower numbers being the thickest and the higher numbers the finest. Their shape is known to everyone, and consists of a simple rod with one end shaped into a hook to take the thread and a flattened shape in the centre which makes it easy to hold between the thumb and finger. The threads include cotton, wool, Courtelle, nylon and silk, and are chosen to suit the work in hand. They are numbered with the higher numbers for the finest work and the lower numbers for heavier work.

It is possible to crochet a variety of articles ranging from frocks, blouses, cushions, table mats, rugs, gloves, hats and berets to edgings, insets, laces and bedspreads.

The origins of this craft are very obscure and probably date back to the time the first thread was spun. It is popular today and very much in vogue at the moment for frocks, waistcoats and 'see-through' blouses. In Italy various characteristic types have evolved. In the Friuli region, for instance, it is worked with a very thick thread and a heavy lace is achieved which is suitable for curtains and rugs, whereas a fine delicate lace, known as Orvieto, has evolved in Umbria.

Here it is used in a fresh way on attractive cushions (page 39). The basic crochet stitches are appliquéd into a finished design. First crochet lengths of chain, braid and fringes, and then apply these to the fabric (with stitches invisible from the right side) creating the design as you work. Here we review the basic crochet stitches, and then give instructions for making the cushions (page 39).

Chain Stitch (see figure 1, left)

This is the simplest and most basic stitch. Make a slip-knot on the hook. Pass the hook under the thread. Catch the thread, draw it up through the loop on the hook making a new loop and allowing the first loop to slip off the hook.

Double Chain Stitch (see figure 2, page 38)

Make a slip-knot on the hook. Chain 2, crochet in the first chain * . By inserting the hook in the left-hand part of the previous double crochet, make a new double crochet *.

Continue repeating from * to *.

Picot Chain (see figure 3, page 38)

Make a slip-knot on the hook. *Chain 4, then Chain 1, pulling the loop to the desired height for Picot. Those on the outer circle of the Sunburst pillow (page 39, middle) measure ¾ inch high. Remove the hook from the Picot loop; insert it in second chain back. Draw thread up making a new stitch; repeat from *.

Ladder Braid (see figures 4, 5 and 6, page 38)

Use cotton or rug wool. Divide the wool into two balls. Then, using a large wooden rug-crocheting needle, make a very loose chain with loops that measure ¾ inch long. Don't cut the wool. (Notice that there are single loops on one side of the chain, crossed loops on the other.) With the other ball of wool and a No. 6 needle, beginning at the single loop side of the first chain, make a slip stitch through each loop until the entire chain has been worked. The chain will shorten up; make more if it is necessary. Now work back down the other side of the chain. This time make slip stitches through the point where loops intersect. While you are working the second side, give a little pull sideways to the original chain. The threads in between should spiral around each other making the ladder.

CUSHIONS

Abstract Cushion (top)
This design, using Chain Stitch, can be any shape you like. Make a large chain by combining several strands of brightly coloured thread. Place the chain on the cushion cover and vary the shapes until you have a pleasing design. Then stitch the chain in place invisibly.

Sunburst Cushion (middle)
Using cotton rug wool, crochet about 2 yards of Chain Stitch. Then, starting at the centre of a cushion cover, stitch the crocheted trim in circles as shown. Make a length of Picot Chain to go around the outside circle.

Striped Cushion (foot)
Yellow and white Chain Stitch, Double Chain Stitch, Ladder Braid and Picot Chain in cotton or rug wool are combined to make this horizontal design on a green background.

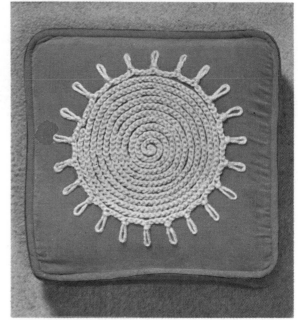

Weaving

The fascination of weaving is in watching a beautifully coloured fabric grow from threads. A beginner's loom such as the one described here is not difficult to make and is an excellent one on which to begin weaving. It is large enough to work placemats, scarves and towels like the ones shown above, or curtains (the last by piecing together widths of the woven fabric to make up the width of curtain required). In this section instructions are given for constructing a simple loom yourself, if you wish. Then we describe the process of warping the loom, or setting up the warp threads. Finally, we show how to build up a fabric on the loom and to complete the weaving.

If you would rather buy a loom, there are many sources and price ranges from which to choose. Be sure the loom is made from hardwood and is sturdily constructed to withstand the pull of the tautly stretched threads and the continuous pounding of the beater.

Assembling the loom

A simple 2-harness loom can be built using the instructions and list of materials given here. Letters show the location of each piece on the drawings (page 41, top) and the instructions refer to the pieces by these letters.

Using the diagram at the top of page 41 as a guide, assemble the right side of the loom frame using two As and two Bs. Drill $\frac{3}{4}$ inch holes through the centre of Bs. Saw a cut 5 inches long at an angle from the top of both B pieces through the holes. Make a crosscut about $2\frac{1}{2}$ inches from the top of both B pieces to make notches. Assemble the frame with notched edges of Bs facing inwards, using lap joints. Fasten with flat-headed wood screws. The inside edges of A should be 5 inches apart.

Next, drill a $\frac{5}{8}$ inch hole through the centre of C, $1\frac{3}{4}$ inches up from the bottom. Cut two $\frac{1}{2}$ inch wide $\frac{3}{8}$ inch deep grooves the length of C, $\frac{1}{2}$ inch in from each side. Centre in frame with the groove facing in. Fasten with screws. (Photograph 1 on page 41.)

For the left side of the loom frame, drill holes only halfway through Bs and C and omit the saw cut and notch in B. Assemble as for right side.

Set frames upright and screw D to C to give correct spacing for warp and cloth beams. Screw E in place and then remove D.

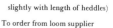

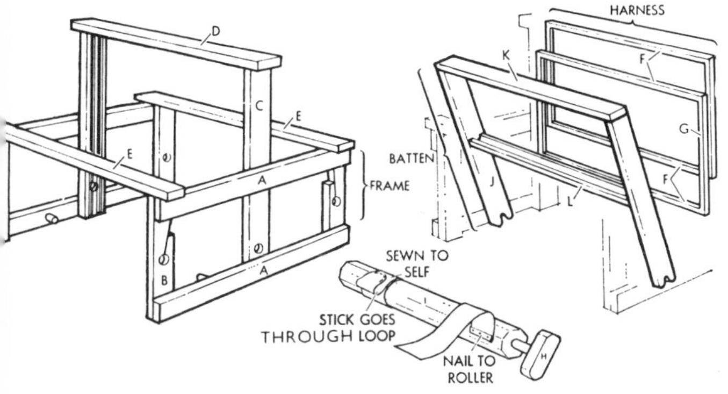

HARNESS

BATTEN
FRAME

D

C

E

A

B

K

F

G

J

L

F

SEWN TO SELF

STICK GOES THROUGH LOOP

NAIL TO ROLLER

Buy 5 foot long 1 × 12 inch. Cut—
A—4 pieces 1½ × 19 inch, top and bottom of loom frame
B—4 pieces 1½ × 8 inch, frame ends
C—2 pieces 2½ × 15 inch, harness guides
D—1 pieces 2½ × 18½ inch, harness guide top
E—2 pieces 1½ × 20 in., warp and cloth beams
H—4 pieces 1½ × 3¼ inch, round-edged knobs
J—2 pieces 1½ × 11½ inch, batten side pieces
K—1 pieces 1½ × 17⅜ inch, batten top
L—1 piece 1½ × 16 inch, batten cross piece
Buy 2 foot long 2 × 4 inch. Cut—
I—2 rollers. Rip 2 × 4 inch in half, cut to 16¼ inch. Cut off corners at 45-degree angle.
Buy 5 foot, ½ × ¾ inch, window stripping. Cut—
F—4 pieces 16½ inch, harness top and bottom
G—4 pieces 8¼ inch, harness ends (may vary

slightly with length of heddles)

To order from loom supplier
15 dent reed, 18 inch long
7 inch metal heddles

Supplies needed
M—⅜ inch diameter dowel 18¾ inch long
N—two ¾ inch dowels 2¼ inch long; 0 two 4 inch long
P—two ⅜ inch diameter dowels 2 inch long
Two 1 × 2 in. carriage bolts; washers; wing nuts
12 inch of ⅛ inch aluminium clothesline wire
Two ⅛ inch screw eyes
28 No. 8 flat-head wood screws 1¼ long
Eight No. 6 round-head wood screws ½ inch long
Sixteen No. 17 brads ½ inch long
Four metal strips 1/16 × ¼ × 16 inch

Assemble the harnesses with F and G, using No. 17 brads. There should be about ⅛ inch space at the top and bottom of the heddles when they are slid on to metal strips and attached to the harness with the round-headed screws placed in notch. (Photograph 2, below.) Slide the harness into place in C.

The next step is making the harness lift mechanism. Drill a ⅝ inch hole through the centre of a block and ⅛ inch holes through each end in line with the ⅝ inch hole. Slide M through the hole in right C, through the block and into the hole in left C. Slide the block to the centre of M. Drill a ⅝ inch hole in the centre of another block and glue this to the free end of M.

Cut the aluminium wire in half and insert in lift knob of dowel. Place small screw eyes in the centre of the lower edge of the harnesses. Slip the other ends of wire into the screw eyes and adjust so that the wires fit snugly; one harness will be up, the other down. Turn the block to force the wires into shape over the dowel. (Photograph 3, below.)

For each roller, drill a ¾ inch hole 1½ inches deep in each end of I. Glue N in one end of I, 1¼ inches from the end, through the centre of the hole. This acts as a key in turning the roller. Insert N in left B. Cut a 1 inch slot in the end of O. Drill a ¾ inch hole in the block and glue O into the knob. Then slide the slotted end of O through the hole in right B and into I. (Photograph 4, below.) Note that the dowels holding the rollers are not glued in place as the rollers must turn freely.

Drill ½ inch holes in right B, midway along saw cut (diagram above). Slide a carriage bolt into the hole with the washer toward the operator. Bolts permit adjustment of pressure on the dowel holding the roller in the correct position for weaving.

Measure 5½ inches back from front edge and drill a ¾ inch hole in lower A on each side. Glue P in each hole to carry batten when it is finished. The last unit of the loom to be made is the batten. Cut ½ inch notches in bottom of J to fit over P. Cut grooves ½ inch wide and ⅜ inch deep in the centre of K and L. Screw together J and K. Cut the reed to fit inside the frame and place top in groove in K. Attach L.

Cut four strips of heavy fabric, such as canvas, 2 inches wide and 8 inches long. Sew a 2 inch loop in one end of each piece. Nail the other end to the rollers, 2 inches in from the ends of each roller. (See sketch above.) From scraps of wood cut two sticks ¼ × ½ × 15 inches. Sand the surface smooth and slip sticks through fabric loops. The warp threads will be tied to these sticks. You will also need to make shuttles and a beater stick from the scrap wood. All should be ¼ × ¾ × 15 inches. Shuttles have a U-shaped notch in each end and the beater stick has one end tapered to a point. All are sanded smooth. For ease of operation keep your loom waxed with paste floor wax.

1

2

3

4

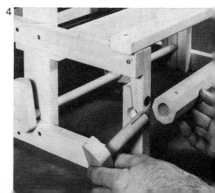

Weaving Instructions

Weaving Instructions

The first process in weaving is warping the loom. When you have completed this, the fabric is half finished.

Decide on the kind of material you want to work with, the colour and the number of yards of fabric you want to make. Firm cotton thread such as carpet weave is a good material with which to begin. To calculate the amount of thread needed, first count the number of spaces in the reed you are using. A loom built from the directions given here will have about 225 spaces. Multiply the number of spaces by the length of material to get the yardage for warp thread.

When you know the amount of yardage needed for warp threads, double this figure and you will find the amount you need for the finished fabric. The first step is to find the number of threads necessary to fill the reed; make each thread the same length by using a warping frame (page 43, top left). The most common kind of frame is a rectangular wooden one that is wide enough so that 1 inch dowel rods set into two sides of the frame are 1 yard apart. The warping frame (page 43, top left) has two extra dowels in the top row placed off-centre to the left.

Suppose you plan to make five yards of fabric. Tie thread around dowel 5 (diagram page 43, top left). Wind thread, as shown in drawing, to dowel 1. Next, wind thread up and over 1 and 1A, and under 1B. Go around 1C, back over 1B, and under 1A. Then wind thread back down to dowel 5 where you began. When you have ten threads wound around dowel rod 1C, tie them together. Each group of ten threads gives a count of twenty threads for a loom since the yardage has been wound up one way and down the other.

To use several colours in the warp, break the thread either where you begin winding (dowel 5) or at dowel 1C. To tie threads together, put the ends together and knot. Be sure to keep the knot close to the end of the peg. Remove any knots found in the thread as you wind; cut the thread back to the beginning or end of the warp and tie on a new piece. Knots in the middle of the warp will show in the finished woven fabric. When you have finished winding the number of threads you

need, break the thread and tie it to dowel 5 where you began winding. Tie a piece of string about 6 inches down the warp from 1A. Cut two straight sticks $\frac{1}{2} \times \frac{1}{2} \times 12$ inches long with holes drilled in each end. These are called lease sticks. Insert one in either side of the cross formed by dowels 1A and 1B. Tie the sticks together at each end through the holes that are drilled there (drawing on page 43, top left).

To take the warp off the frame, begin at dowel 5. Slip threads off the peg while grasping warp firmly about 12 inches from the end. The first tie near the peg makes the beginning loop, through which another length of warp is drawn, like chain crochet. Draw up the loops until you reach the lease sticks.

Tie the lease sticks firmly at both ends to the cloth beam of loom with short end of chain facing into loom. Remove heddles from the frames by bowing bars out of the screws holding them to harnesses. Starting at the right end of groups of threads, pick out the first thread.

Push this loop through the next to last slot in the reed. A reed hook or slim crochet hook will help. Pull the thread through the reed and put it over one end of the stick that is inserted in the cloth holders on the other side of the loom (see page 42, lower photograph).

Take up the next thread and, skipping one slot, insert it into the second free slot. Continue in this manner across the reed using every other slot (the only exception is a fine thread which is put through double in the reed; in that case, use every slot).

When the reed is threaded, slip on the other cloth holder and begin winding the warp on to the warp roller. Wind clockwise so that the threads go under the roller and around (page 42, top photograph).

Wind only a little at a time, until you feel the

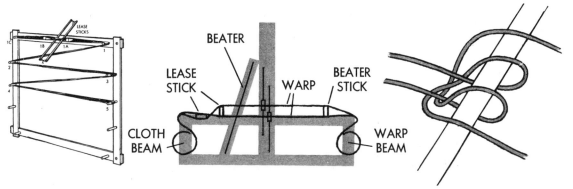

warp tense. Do not pull too tightly or you will break the threads. Tighten the carriage bolts when you stop. A flat stick with a tapered end (a beater stick) helps loosen the knots and pull the warp straight. Use the stick to beat the warp as you would a carpet.

If the loom is placed on a table so that the chained warp falls loosely to the floor, the weight of material keeps the tension even. Insert paper into the warp beam roller as you roll up the warp to keep different levels of thread from matting. Be sure the sides do not slip off the paper, as they will be shorter than the middle of the warp and cause the fabric to be crooked.

Stop rolling when the ends of the threads are about 5 inches from the lease sticks. Tighten down the warp beam. Cut off the ends of the threads to the same size as the shortest end. A small difference in thread length is normal but if there is a difference of 6 inches or more, it would be wise to re-roll your material. Cut the threads holding the lease stick to the cloth beam but hold them tightly at the end so that they do not slip. Set the stick closest to the reed on the edge. Half the threads are on the top edge and half fall below. Carefully edge the stick up toward the beater. Pull the warp tightly.

Looking through the warp from the side, you will see the 'shed' which continues through the reed and into the back of the loom. Put the beater stick through the shed. Make sure it corresponds exactly to the stick in front and that there are no tangled threads in the middle. Turn the beater stick on end (see diagram page 43, top centre). Slip out the lease stick (just the one) and put it back next to the beater stick. Make sure they lie on the same threads. Slip out the beater stick and repeat with the remaining front lease stick.

Starting again from the right side of the loom, count off twenty threads and pull them out of the reed. Tie with a loose slip-knot. Continue across the warp, tying each group of twenty. Put the heddles back into frames on the loom. Because of crossed threads still held by lease sticks, you will be able to locate the first thread at the right of the warp. Put thread through the eye of the first heddle in the front harness. Take up second thread. Put it through the eye of the first heddle in the back harness (photograph page 43, bottom). Notice how one thread goes over one lease stick and under the other, and the second thread is just the reverse.

Check as you repeat the process across the loom to be sure that the threads are in order. Re-tie the threads in twenties as you cross the loom and let the ends drop.

The last step is putting threads back into the

reed. Put one thread through every space since threads are now single. (If you are threading double with fine thread, put two in a space.) Start again at the right and repeat across.

Tie groups of twenty threads to the stick which fits in the cloth on the roller in this manner; divide group of twenty into groups of ten. Holding the groups apart, tie as shown in the diagram page 43, top right. This is a weaver's knot and will hold your material securely. Make sure the tension across the warp is even. Re-tie the groups if necessary to guarantee even tension.

When all the threads are tied down, tighten the cloth beam until the tension is firm and tighten the wing nut. Cut threads off the lease sticks.

Building a Fabric

When the warping is finished, you are ready for the most enjoyable part of weaving — building a fabric. Here are directions for plain and fancy weaving and for finishing your fabric. The fabrics shown in the photograph (page 45, right) are: plain (A); plaid (B); leno (C); laid-in design (D).

Any of these weaves can be mastered on a loom that you have built yourself or on a simple loom that has been purchased.

Once the warping is finished, half the threads are in place. After the threads are tied on the loom, tighten them down by leaving the front wing nut secured, while releasing the back nut and turning the back roller until the threads are taut but not tense.

Pull the side lever towards you. Insert one of the lease sticks against which to beat the first thread. Insert the shuttle (page 44, bottom right), which should be already wound, and push it through to the other side, leaving an end twice the width of your fabric. Beat the thread down with the batten. Change to shed B by turning the side lever away from you. Beat the first thread once again. Insert the shuttle; push it through. That is all there is to basic or 'tabby' weaving.

The shuttles should be almost as wide as the material you are making. You will need three or four if you use several colours. They can be made from scraps of wood but must be sanded until they are very smooth so that they won't catch on threads as they are pushed through the shed. To wind a shuttle, wrap the thread around one end to hold it; then bring the thread under the top

end and under the bottom end in a figure 8 motion (page 44, bottom right). To add a new colour, as for plaid, (page 45, top left), cut off the old colour at either end of a row, leaving an end about 2 inches long. When the shed is changed for the next row, put this end that is left through six or eight threads. It will be in the same shed as the new colour. Put the second colour through and leave a 2 inch end which is doubled back on the next shed. The little tag ends can be cut off after the fabric has been washed.

After weaving two or three inches of material, finish off the beginning edge of the fabric. The same method is used for finishing off at the end of the fabric or between pieces on the loom.

Thread the long end left at the beginning of the fabric into a blunt tapestry needle. Go under the first four threads on the loom, up and over the same threads, then under again. Bring the needle from underneath and through the fabric between the second and third rows. This is step 1 of the finishing-off process.

For step 2, put the needle under the next four threads and up between second and third rows. Do not go around the threads, just go under them. Going across the row, go around the threads twice (step 1) at the start. Work step 2 four times, then step 1 once, step 2 four times, and continue this pattern. At the other end of the fabric, work step 2 twice and then fasten the thread (page 45, 2 left). Watch selvages of the fabric closely. If you pull thread too tightly, the edges will be drawn in unevenly. It will take a bit of practice to make the edges just right, but this is the mark of a good weaver.

When the completed material gets close to the batten, move it down by releasing the warp and cloth beams. Turn the cloth beam, pulling newly woven material under the beam. Tighten the back nut. Pull the material so that it is taut, and then tighten the front catch.

Now you can move on to some fancy stitches. First, take 'leno' weave. It makes a lacy path across the plain or 'tabby' weave. Work back and forth three or five times across an inch of warp. Then pick up three of the threads from the bottom row of threads and bring them above the top row of threads.

Now bring your finger between the bottom three threads and the next top three threads and let the top threads drop below your finger. The shuttle

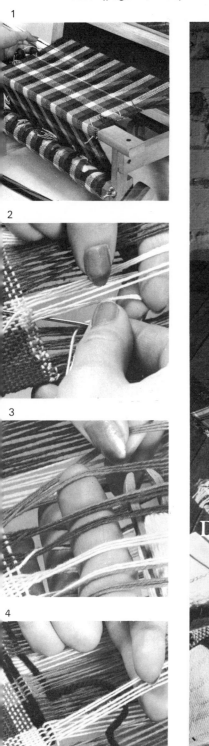

1

2

3

4

should follow the new 'shed' made with the fingers. Continue across the row. Weave the last inch plain. Change the shed and throw the shuttle plain for one shot. Repeat twist, throw the shuttle, and continue with plain weave.

To weave in a monogram, or practically any pattern which can be drawn on graph paper, use the 'laid-in' technique. Using a contrasting coloured thread (it can be heavier as well), introduce it into the shed, bringing one end up and over the top threads where the new colour is to appear. In the same shed throw the shuttle through, and beat as usual (page 45, 4 left).

On the next shed, pick up the contrasting thread and bring it up and over the top threads, widening or narrowing the colour area as you choose.

Throw the shuttle through again on the same shed. You can work out an endless variety of designs. It is best to work your design out on graph paper before you begin weaving it; that way you can avoid mistakes or an unattractive pattern.

If you are interested in learning more about weaving and other stitches you can use, there are many excellent books that provide more details and instructions.

45

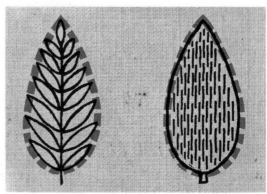

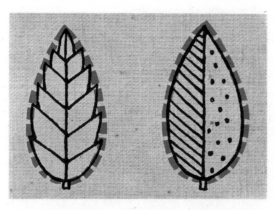

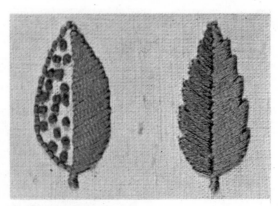

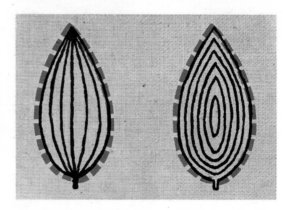

Embroidery

This section on embroidery is designed to help the beginner to master a number of stitches, which can then be applied to almost anything, clothes, mats, cushions or table linen.

The following explanations of commonly used terms may help embroidery beginners.

Traced design
Designs are outlined on the fabric which can be bought ready for embroidering. Generally, a guide to the colours to be used is enclosed with these bought embroidery kits.

Counted design
This means that evenly woven fabric is used and a chart provided so that the design can be counted on the threads of the fabric.

Transfer designs
These kits include fabric and a transfer with working instructions. The impression of the design is ironed on to the fabric.

Needlework packs
These can be bought containing traced fabric,

chart or transfer designs along with the required working materials.

EMBROIDERY STITCHES

The leaf designs shown on page 46 illustrate how the same shape (see dotted lines) can be varied by using different stitches. The stitches illustrated here are very easy to achieve. Before tackling the finished piece of embroidery, practise the stitches on a similar piece of material and assess the necessary weight of thread. This is easily adjusted if stranded cotton is being used, as the weight can be varied from one to six strands. Sometimes a thread like Coton-à-broder makes a neater stitch than stranded cotton and sometimes a much heavier weight such as Soft Embroidery thread, rug wool, raffia or even string is necessary to achieve the desired effect. Interesting results can be obtained by using different weights together.

Stem and Crewel Stitch
This stitch is illustrated in Figure A (below). Stem stitches are used to define lines, or in parallel rows to fill an area. Anchor the thread so as to work away from you. Continue the stitch until the line or area is filled.

Long and Short Stitch
This stitch is shown in Figure B (below). The first row of the stitches is made of one short and one long stitch alternately. The following rows are worked in stitches all the same length. This is a form of Satin stitch (see below) that is used for shading and texture. The length of the stitch is adjusted to fit the outside contour of the design.

Satin Stitch
This stitch is shown in Figure C (below) and is probably the best known of the 'filling' stitches used to cover large areas in a hurry. The thread is carried across an area in parallel stitches, returning underneath the fabric. Be sure that the needle is slightly more slanted in the return stitch and keep the straight stitches close together to fill in the design.

Seeding
This, illustrated in Figure D, is a simple filling stitch that is composed of small straight stitches of equal size which are placed at random over the surface of the design as shown. Use this stitch for light filling of large areas such as flowers or leaves where a solid effect is not needed. It takes some practice to make it even, so try it out on a sample of fabric first.

Rumanian Stitch
Shown in Figure E, this stitch is usually put to work filling a leaf or flower. It is worked from top to bottom. Bring the thread through at the top left of the shape; carry the thread across and take a stitch on the right side of the shape with the thread below the needle (first diagram). Take a stitch at the left side, with the thread above the needle (second diagram).

These two movements are worked until the shape is filled. Keep the stitches close together for the most finished look. The size of the centre crossing stitch can be varied, either to make a long oblique stitch or a small stitch that is straight. By varying the size of the centre crossing stitch, you can actually alter the appearance of the design itself. It is as well to practice this on a sample of fabric before proceeding.

Straight Stitch
This stitch (Figure F) is a series of single-spaced stitches worked in either a regular or irregular manner. Sometimes they are of varying size. The stitches should be neither too long nor too loose. The Straight stitch, one of the easiest stitches to master, is ideal for flower outlines and other simple design effects on wall hangings or samplers.

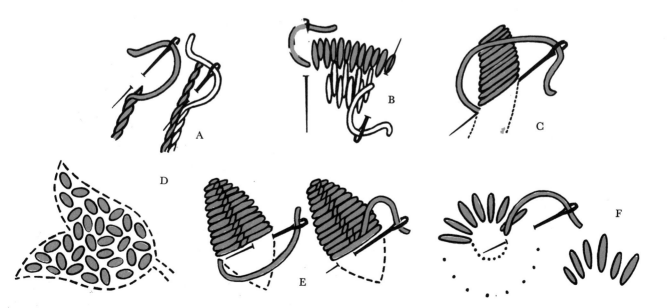

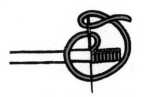

French Knot

Bring the needle up through the fabric; hold tip of the needle close to the point. Wrap thread over it one or more times, depending upon the size of knot required. Hold the thread taut by placing your thumb at 'X' position (shown above). Swing the needle in the direction of the arrow. Push it down through the dot where the first stitch was taken. Pull the needle and thread through to under side, forming a knot.

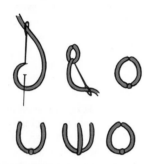

Lazy Daisy Stitch

Make the versatile stitch shown above similar to the Chain stitch illustrated on page 49, but after each loop is completed, make a small stitch to secure it neatly in its place. Make all Lazy Daisy stitches the same length, but vary the centre, securing stitch to any length to achieve different effects. Also vary the outside stitches as much as necessary, as suggested in the second line above.

Blanket Stitch

Insert the needle up through the fabric, going under the upper thread forming a loop as shown above. Continue making over and under stitches as long as necessary and in any direction.

Threaded Running Stitch

The stitch is worked horizontally, from right to left: two or three threads are taken up passing over five or six. The length of the stitch may be varied according to the effect desired. A second thread, sometimes of a different colour, is passed above and below the line of stitching.

Buttonhole Stitch

Make a Running stitch along line to be buttonholed; then overcast along the line, working from right to left, as indicated in the diagram above.

Cretan Stitch

To start the stitch, pull the thread through the fabric near the top. Your starting point will mark the beginning of the row of stitches. Carry the thread around to the front and pass the needle under a few threads of fabric on a horizontal line in a little below the starting point. The needle will be turned towards the centre, carried across the slack thread. Make a similar stitch on the left side of the starting stitch, with the needle point back to right as shown above.

The third Cretan stitch is on the right side of centre. The needle must be drawn across the slack thread each time to produce the desired twisted effect.

When working from top to bottom (you can work from side to side), each stitch must be taken somewhat below the one just made on the other side of the centre line, rather than opposite it.

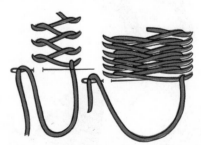

The basic Cretan stitch is varied by changing the length of stitches on each side of the centre line, and/or the width between them.

Chain Stitch

To make Chain stitch, bring the needle with thread to the front side of the fabric; hold the thread to form a loop. The needle should enter the fabric where the thread of the previous stitch came through. Go over the thread loop to complete the stitch.

Algerian Eye Stitch

Each star or eye consists of eight stitches that are all taken around a central point. Arrange the stitches in a square. For variation, use one colour of thread for the horizontal and vertical lines, another colour for the diagonal lines.

Couching Stitch

Use Couching stitch as an outline stitch or to secure other threads. Lay the heavy thread to be couched on top of the fabric, shaping it to follow the design line. Pin the wool or thread in place to secure it before you start Couching stitches.

If the wool is not too heavy, thread the needle and pull it through the fabric to anchor the one end. Pull the needle holding finer wool through the material close to the couching wool.

Next, make a series of vertical stitches over the couching thread and through the fabric to the under side. In order to make the stitches vertical on the front side of fabric, the needle must go through to the underneath of the fabric in a diagonal direction. The stitch may be performed from right to left as illustrated, from left to right, or up and down.

The length of the stitches may be varied for decorative effect.

Cross Stitch

This stitch can be started at either the right or the left of the area to be decorated. To begin, make a row of slanted stitches equal in length and evenly spaced. Then, work back over them in the opposite direction. This makes a row of Cross stitches. The reverse side will show a row of upright stitches.

Feather Stitch

With the thread under a slanted needle, make a Blanket stitch to the right of a straight perpendicular line. With the thread under the needle, make the Blanket stitch to the left. Repeat. A fancy Feather stitch is made by working several stitches on each side. They may be evenly spaced or grouped.

A further variation is made by pointing the needle straight down so the outside stitches are parallel and closed.

EMBROIDERY FRAMES

There are several sizes of circular embroidery frames on sale in craft-shops, varying from approximately 3 to 10 inches in diameter.

'Line' stitches such as Chain, Stem, Back and Coral stitch are more easily done in the hand, but for counted thread methods of embroidery such as Black work and Canvas work, a frame is a great help, and for Drawn Thread work and Drawn Fabric the frame is definitely a 'must'.

Mounting

Each piece of needlework to be mounted, and particularly those not done on a frame, must be stretched. This can be done professionally or at home (your nearest needlework shop will be able to supply booklets containing instructions for this).

Completed decorative panels must be mounted and framed very carefully. A piece of heavy cardboard or thin plywood is necessary to stretch the material on. This must be just slightly smaller than the actual frame to allow for the thickness of the material. The centres should be marked on all four sides of both the embroidery and the backing. With the embroidery face down on the table and all centre marks matching, a Herring-bone stitch should be used to catch the edges together, working first from side to side and then from top to bottom stretching all the while and always working outwards from the centre. When the stretching is complete, the frame is placed face down and the embroidery put into position within it.

Tenerife

Tenerife embroidery was probably developed from Tenerife lace, a form of needle-made lace known in South and Central America as Brazilian or Bolivian lace. It is reported to be an imitation of 'Sols' (Sun-lace) executed in Spain in the 16th and 17th centuries. It is very delicate and consists of various forms of rosettes made on stretched threads.

Although the designs are simple they must be executed with care as it is very difficult to unpick the work once it is finished. First the design must be drawn on tracing linen; it is made up of circles, semi-circles and straight lines radiating from the centre. The drawing is then transferred to thin card which will keep the embroidery stretched while it is being executed. The drawing is then outlined with Running stitches, the stitch alternately bridging and skipping the spaces between the radii. A thread is attached to one of the Running stitches and taken across the diameter of the circle and threaded through the opposite stitch. This process is repeated by coming back through the

nearest stitch across the circle to take up the opposite stitch and continuing thus, the thread passing twice through each Running stitch until the circle is filled with rays. The pattern is worked on the web so made in various different stitches. Darning stitch, cording, webs, knots are all used in this kind of lace-making. Cording consists of whipping two or more of the radii together. The webs are made quite simply by using darning stitch over and under the radii. The knot stitch is more complicated and consists of gathering the desired number of radii threads together with the needle, bringing the needle to the right side of the material under the loop so formed and pulling the threads together.

Originally, Tenerife lace was worked on small round or square pillows covered with a firm cloth on to which the design was traced. Steel pins were placed, points facing the centre, all around the outside circumference of the design at the tip of each radiating line. Starting from the centre, the

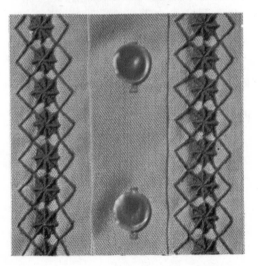

thread was taken from one pin to that exactly opposite on the diameter, until the circle was filled as has been described in the previous method.

Later, special circular hinged metal frames were made with saw-toothed edges. These were made in all shapes and sizes and a hinge allowed the work to be removed on completion.

Both the lace and embroidery are worked in the same way from the centre out, like a spider's web. To give a three-dimensional look to the embroidery, pearl cotton is used instead of the ordinary embroidery thread.

Tenerife can be used effectively to trim plain garments; or for household linen, guest towels, pillowcases, napkins, table runners, or dinner mats. Place pinwheels done in Tenerife embroidery (see below, foot) at random on the fabric or trimming edges, varying the colours for a finished rainbow effect, or make a Tenerife border such as that shown below. Complete instructions are given for these designs.

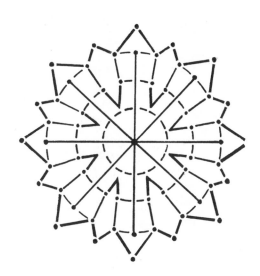

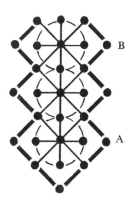

Tenerife Rings

Materials

1 ball pearl cotton. No. 20 tapestry needle.

Instructions

Trace the diagram (page 51, foot) and transfer it to stiff paper or light cardboard. Then, holding the pattern in place on the fabric with a pin through the centre dot of the diagram, pierce each dot with the tapestry needle, and mark the dots in pencil on the fabric.

With long Straight stitches make an 8-stitch web radiating from the centre. For the outer web, make two $\frac{1}{4}$ inch Straight stitches between each stitch of the 8-stitch web (see page 51, top left) to meet the third dotted line. Weave under and over the webs alternately on the right side only, bringing the weaving threads close together. Starting at any stitch in the centre, weave over the centre web to within the first dotted line. Then work over the 3-stitch web from the second dotted line to within the third dotted line.

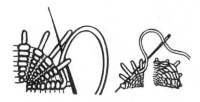

Following the heavy lines on the diagram, work first the outer zigzag line, then work the V stitches between the inner and outer webs.

Repeat for each ring.

Tenerife Border

Materials

1 ball pearl cotton. No. 20 tapestry needle.

Instructions

The diagram below shows a set of three motifs (from A to B). To make a border, repeat the pattern from A to B as many times as required.

Trace the pattern on stiff paper or light cardboard. Then, having placed the pattern on the fabric, pierce each dot of the pattern with the tapestry needle and mark the dots with a pencil on the fabric. Be sure to keep the motifs straight.

With long Straight stitches, make an 8-stitch web radiating from the centre as shown (page 51, top right). Weave over the web on the right side only, bringing the weaving threads close together. Starting at any stitch at the centre on the first motif, weave in and out over the 8-stitch web to within the dotted line. Work other motifs the same way. Make a zigzag line around each border in Straight stitches.

Embroidered Wall Hangings

Wall hangings can add a very personal touch to a room if you design them yourself using your own colour scheme. Simplified shapes are a necessity and the proportions of the design should take into consideration the wall space available. Materials

are limitless and may include metal, wire, glass, shells, threads, string, cords and raffia.

Some embroideries may become slightly warped in the making and will require stretching back into shape. The embroidery should be damped and stretched into its correct shape and pinned out over layers of damp blotting-paper to dry.

The colourful wall hangings, some modern, some traditional, shown on pages 52–5, will give you a chance to apply your embroidery skills and create original decorations for your home. Using the ideas in this section, you can make your own designs.

Flower and leaf motifs decorate the contemporary wall hanging (page 52, left), which has a background of felt. Here, rectangular pieces are sewn on, and the designs embroidered over them.

Felt birds over a colourful flower tree and sprightly green grass (page 52, right) make up this modern design where the shapes are appliquéd to the backing.

The gold hanging with a more traditional design (page 53, left) is woven, with a satin lining. The design is a combination of wavy lines and flowers.

The vivid maroon and purple hanging (page 53, right) has a corduroy backing and is decorated with tapestry wools and crochet thread.

Ideal for a sampler, the abstract design in golds and browns (page 54) is developed in a free-style way from repeated embroidery stitches in threads of various textures.

Finally, the colourful flower composition (page 55) is suitable for a bedroom, or any room where a special touch of colour is needed. It is made in hessian, with felt flowers.

On pages 54 and 55 are full instructions for making all these wall hangings giving colours and materials.

Contemporary Wall Hanging

For this design (page 52, left) choose grey felt 20 × 56 inches for the background. The space is broken with an elongated rectangle of light pink felt, with a small bright green felt rectangle superimposed on it. Bright green is used again for the rectangle at the top left.

Another rectangular shape is in red; while a dark purple rectangle, with one corner rounded, another cut out, is placed at the bottom right of the hanging.

The pieces should be placed in position, pinned securely, then tacked to hold. Using two strands of embroidery thread, buttonhole each piece to the background. The long line in the centre is crocheted in deep pink wool. First work a chain the necessary length, in single crochet (see instructions on page 39), then two rows of treble stitch. Fasten this to the background with Running stitch in contrasting coloured embroidery thread. When the chain is in position, pin 1 inch long loops of wool in position and secure with Couching stitch.

Flower loops are shaped by hand, pinned in place and held with Couching stitch worked with two strands of thread. Stems for the rosettes on the red felt are two strands of wool, pinned, then couched in place. Flower centres are small bundles of wool tied in the centre with a long piece of thinner wool, the ends all pulled through

and tied off at the back. Some are clipped to form balls, others are left with the loops showing.

Solid flower centres are made by coiling wool into a flat spiral, pinning in position, then couching with two strands of thread. Loops around the spirals are pinned, then couched.

The main stem of the plant on the green felt is made of single and treble crochet; the side stems are single crochet. Leaves are pinned in place and secured with Couching stitches.

Modern Design with Birds and Tree

For this (page 52, right) the background of homespun fabric measures 20 × 56 inches with a 3 inch slot for a wooden slat at the top and a 5½ inch wide hem at the bottom. In spite of its size, this hanging is light enough to go easily on any wall.

Cut out birds of red and/or orange and black felt measuring about 3 × 2½ inches each. Tack the birds to the background by hand with fine stitches, half facing one way, half facing the other, with wings tilted at a flying angle. Finish off with embroidered eyes, beaks and top-knots.

The tree stands about 28 inches high. Its trunk and branches of purple felt are blanket-stitched to backing. The flowers range from 1½ inches to 4 inches in diameter; attach the larger of these and some small ones to the backing with Blanket stitches; attach the smaller ones at the centre only. Others can be secured by couched coils of wool. At the centre of each flower, stitch clipped and unclipped tassels. The tiny felt flowers and green stems at the base of the tree are hand-tacked in position with fine stitches.

Gold Hanging

This hanging (page 53, left) has a satin lining and outside measurements of 12 × 36 inches. The fabric shown is woven, but any heavy-body material would do equally well.

Lazy Daisy and Cross stitches are combined to work flowers in multi-coloured thread. French Knots provide centres for each of the flowers. The wavy lines are fine Running stitches of royal blue crochet thread laced with purple or blue thread. The spaces between flowers are dotted with French Knots. The wall hanging is then lined with a soft, gold satin using a simple hemming stitch. It would also make a luxurious stole.

Maroon and Purple Hanging

This hanging (page 53, right) has corduroy framing a background of men's suit interlining and is attached to denim lining all round.

The corduroy pieces of maroon, purple, black and blue in the design are appliquéd with Blanket stitches. Feather stitches are used to finish the border. Each of the flowers and leaves is made from a separate piece of interlining, cut out, finished with Blanket stitches, and then tacked securely by hand.

The leaf shapes have Chain stitching for veins. Some are accented by French Knots, others by Lazy Daisy stitches. For the rippled flowers, Cretan stitches are combined with French Knots or Chain stitches with French Knots and Lazy Daisy stitches. By interchanging crochet thread and wool often, it is possible to vary texture, colour and depth delightfully in the wall hanging. Any closely related colour scheme may be used to achieve this effect.

This modern hanging (page 54) is created by means of repeated embroidery stitches, ranging from fairly simple ones at the top, to rather more complex ones, like Couching, towards the bottom.

To adapt this idea, you will need a piece of coarse linen, assorted threads and wools, some string and perhaps even rope.

Allow ½ inch all round the design for framing.

Flower Composition

The design (page 55) is worked on a natural-coloured hessian ground, with green, red and blue felt shapes and embroidery. Vary the weight of thread from 2 to 6 strands to add more interest.

Make a border of royal blue Running stitch, accented with a scallop lacing. Tiny birds are made from scraps of felt, with triangular orange bodies and round red heads, appliquéd with blue Blanket stitch. Their eyes are blue French Knots. The stems and leaves are green felt, appliquéd to the background with various colours of thread.

Orange felt makes the flowers and buds, trimmed with royal blue felt circles, then edged with royal blue French Knots. The flowers are surface-decorated with Lazy Daisy stitches. The finished size is about 13 × 16 inches.

Gifts for Children

Imagination and humour are combined to make up these wall hangings for children, the friendly lion (above), the stylized sandpipers (page 57, right) and the purple cat (page 57, foot); and the imposing toy chest (above).

Toy Chest

The toy chest (page 56) uses leftover wood. Cut six plywood rectangles, two pieces 26 × 22 inch for front and back, two 20 × 22 inch for sides and two 20 × 26 inch for top and bottom. Fasten with fine nails, fitting edges and corners neatly. Screw hinges so that lid can open a full 270°.

For decoration glue on 1 inch thick wood blocks and 1 × 2 inch strips, nail firmly in place. Centre front panel may have an initial carved in relief and the chest should be stained.

Lion Hanging

The lion (opposite) is stitched on to cotton ticking that has been tightly stretched on a wooden frame. Sketch your design on paper and transfer this to the background with coloured waxed carbon paper.

The mane, tail and beard are done in loops of inexpensive rug wool, the body is in Long and Short stitch in wool, and lightweight black wool outlines the figure in Stem stitch.

The butterfly is chain-stitched in pretty colours of lightweight wool.

This panel needs no framing. The ticking background is taken to the back of the panel, mitred at the corners and laced with strong thread as explained on page 50 using Herring-bone stitch.

Sandpipers

The sandpipers in this wall hanging are first cut out of hessian, then appliquéd to the backing with wool. The rather casual finish to the outlines of these birds gives them a very distinct character. The beaks, legs and butterfly are chain-stitched. In size the two larger birds measure 10 × 6½ inches and 9½ × 9½ inches; the others are 6 × 3½ inches, 9 × 6 inches and 7 × 5½ inches.

The background is hessian and measures 17½ × 39 inches. The panel hangs from a wooden dowel laced through six loops of hessian which are made by folding the fabric into 1 inch wide bands measuring 3 inches from end to end. Heavy cotton material is used to line the loops and to back the panel.

Purple Cat

This amusing cat is embroidered on textured linen or hessian stretched on plywood and backed with a wooden panel covered with material.

Outline the cat's body, tail, head and ears with a Pekinese stitch, which can be repeated on small areas within the cat.

Fill in other areas with Running stitches, Satin stitch, and French Knots (page 49). The smooth solid effect on the cheeks, around the eyes and inside the body is achieved by Seeding (page 49). Appliqué small patches of felt for the fish, the ears, the nose and the squares inside the body. Pipe cleaners will make very satisfactory whiskers.

Fabric Collages

The enormous variety of handicraft materials available—plastics, brilliant papers and paints, all the efficient protective sprays and handy tools— makes it possible for you to design and create whatever you please, such as these attractive fabric collages, the wool hanging (above) and the amusing stylized cats (page 59). Full instructions are given below.

For a fabric collage, you will need scissors and fabric, fabric glue from an art shop, iron-on Vilene or photographic mountant paper from an art or photographic shop, and hardboard. If photographic mountant paper is placed between two pieces of paper and ironed with a warm iron, the two layers of paper are firmly stuck together. Sketches, illustrations, cut-outs and photos can all be mounted in this way.

First, determine the size you want the hanging to be and have hardboard cut to that size. Cut the background fabric to measure, apply an inch of fabric glue to your board at the top and anchor the background firmly. Roll the remaining fabric forward, glueing and attaching about 4 inches at a time. When the background is firm and dry you are ready to apply the design.

Outline Wool Bird Hanging

This hanging uses embroidery thread or wool which can either be stitched or glued. In this wool wall hanging, hessian is stapled on to a piece of heavy card for the background. When the hessian is taut arrange strands of wool, using two or more closely related colours, in a pleasing design on the front and glue down. Make sure that you glue a small portion of the design at a time in order to keep the pattern intact. If the embroidery is executed in thread or wool and stuck to the background it is not necessary to worry about finishing the ends neatly. The glue will prevent any ends from fraying and so the threads are simply cut where the design necessitates. If the design is to be stitched, however, the thread must be couched and all ends taken to the back of the work and fastened firmly into the backs of the stitches. Couching is an easy and very effective method of achieving a bold result. A fairly heavy thread is laid for the outline and a lighter weight thread stitched across it to hold it in position. Sometimes a simple Straight stitch is used at right angles to the laid thread or perhaps Cross stitch, grouped Satin stitch or Gloving stitch. Rug wool, cords of various thicknesses, coloured string or even raffia could be used for either the glued or embroidered method.

Stylized Cats

Brilliant colours and patterned materials make these cats an attractive and amusing collage. The heads are half-circles of fabric, the bodies and legs are shaped rectangles, and the ears and claws are triangles, as are the birds perched on the back of one of the cats.

The various fabric pieces for the designs are attached individually to the background fabric with iron-on interfacing or photographic mountant paper. First of all, back each design piece by placing the wrong side of your design fabric on the interfacing or photographic paper and lightly touching the centre of each shape with a warm iron until the fabric sticks to the paper. Then, cut out the shape. Repeat for each of the design pieces you will need. You will find that, as you cut, the action of the scissors will bond the edges of the mountant and fabric.

Now place the backed design pieces one by one on the background fabric, following the order in which they are on the design. To attach a design piece to the background, place the bonded piece in its exact position on the collage. Cover it with tissue paper to avoid direct contact with heat and press carefully with a warm iron. Work slowly and easily, avoiding wrinkles in the fabric, iron over the surface of the design, using a little pressure on the edges of the fabric piece.

The blue details suggesting eyes, whiskers and the bow on the tail should be attached to the shapes before they are mounted, using exactly the same method as has been already described.

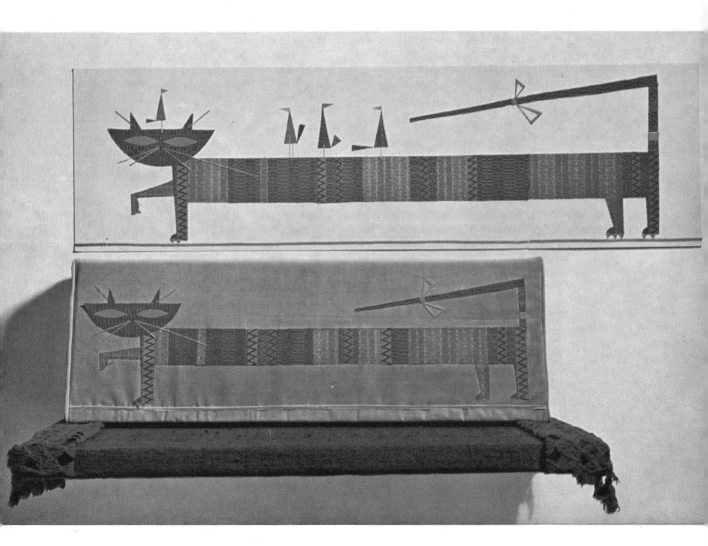

Origami

This fascinating pastime of paper folding comes from Japan, where children learn it at school. Step-by-step directions for making the charming geisha doll are shown below.

Geisha Doll

For a 12 inch doll, cut a piece of white tissue paper 9 inches wide and 12 inches long. Roll it around a pencil and push the paper down until it wrinkles tightly (see Figure 1, below). Repeat with 2 × 9 inch and 1½ × 9 inch pieces of tissue paper. Then lay the string across the large piece of paper and roll it to within 4 inches of the end, stuffing it with cotton (Figure 2). Put cotton wool in the small pieces of tissue as well, fold over and tie as shown (Figure 3). Now place the small rolls inside the larger, with a piece of colourful print paper between the small rolls, and then tie. Stuff cotton wool in the ruffle of paper under the roll at the front, and tie to form the face and neck (Figure 4).

Next you need a piece of flowered paper 8 × 10 inches. Fold back 1 inch at the top, then bring 1 inch back over to the front (Figure 5). Lay the doll's head on this paper and fold as shown (Figure 6). Repeat this last process with some coloured or patterned paper. For the *obi* (or sash), paste a 1 × 5 inch strip of printed paper around the figure. Then, to form bow-like ends, fold in half a 2 × 5 inch strip of the same paper, wrap a ½ inch wide strip around it (Figure 7), and then paste this at the back so only the ends can be seen from the front. The geisha's hair is painted with black tempera paint. Dolls of all sizes are obvious subjects for this craft. Birds, beasts, fish, trees and flowers may also be attempted.

A varied collection of papers is necessary: cartridge paper of various weights, typing paper, tissue papers in different colours and a selection of patterned papers. There are quite a number of satisfactory quick-setting glues to be chosen from in the craft shops, which help to give a neat and tidy finish. Poster colours are easy and effective to use for any colour scheme. Sharp scissors, a Stanley knife, a bone folder and steel rule are the really necessary tools, but a pair of compasses and a protractor will probably be useful. This is a fascinating craft to develop especially if there are any children in the home to appreciate these delicate toys, also to be treasured as ornaments. A little practice is necessary in handling, folding, or rolling the paper and a little patience in acquiring the craftsman's deftness of touch and sense of colour.

Books on the subject can be borrowed from most libraries or obtained from craft shops. The bone folder and steel rule are probably the most important of the tools. It is impossible to obtain a crisp line without them. The metal rule should be laid along any line which needs a sharp fold. The bone folder is pressed firmly into the paper and against the rule and, while the rule is still in position, the paper is lifted up against it. Special non-slip rules are sold in craft shops for this purpose. They are shaped with a groove along their length so that the thumb and forefinger can hold them firmly in position.

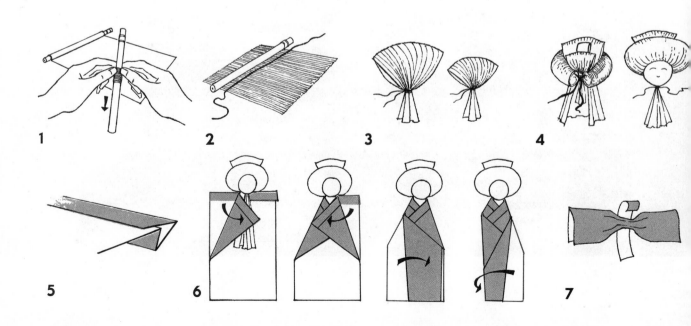

1   2   3   4

5   6   7

Paper Designs

In this section we show how to make colourful designs from paper, the orange and yellow flower collage (left) and the 'stained glass' panels (right); the coffee tin (right) which could be used as a vase or wastepaper basket, uses the same techniques as the panels. Page 63 explains the making of paper flowers and general cutting techniques

for overlay mosaics; you can apply these in your own way to create your own designs.

The designs of the stained glass panels (above) are formed by brilliantly coloured triangles (and other basic shapes) of tissue paper, overlaid on each other. First, cover a piece of glass with the desired base colour of tissue; apply with a clear lacquer spray. Lay on the required shapes, one at a time, and secure with spray. Smooth the surface with your fingers and, when you are sure that your design is dry, trim the edges.

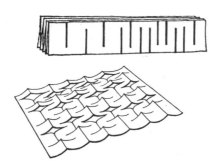

A criss-cross pattern of brightly coloured tissue strips applied vertically, then horizontally, covers a large coffee tin. Finish off the edges of the can at the top and bottom with gay ribbon.

The cutting techniques described here could not be simpler, yet add a professional look to the finished product. First try cutting experiments with three basic shapes, creating abstract shapes from them.

Cut a circle into straight-line sections (below left) without adding to or subtracting from the basic form. After you have done this, move the pieces to expand them into a cut-apart shape. When the proportions of the extended circle please you, paste it on white paper.

A little variation in the basic shape will create a different finished design. An oval expands into a longer and more graceful design after it has been cut.

Rectangles and squares (above right) offer endless possibilities for abstract designs. Gradually, as you cut and work with arrangements from several rectangles, try moving the forms just a little out of their original relationship. The resulting design will still look related, yet be more interesting.

For the best results, cut regular, long shapes in preference to short choppy pieces; the latter are seldom as pleasing to the eye.

Triangles (below right) are the secret behind many of the most effective designs cut from paper. When cutting triangles, manipulate the scissors to produce graceful, curved lines. By moving the pieces out of context slightly you will find fluid lines appearing within the still recognizable triangular shape.

Designs of this sort achieve a beauty peculiar to themselves through use of the unexpected. Try out more than one basic shape and more than one shade in a single design, making sure as you go along that the effect is what you want. Practice will help you to develop an eye for pattern.

Inexpensive papers in rainbow colours can be used to decorate trays, make pictures, or cover tins of various shapes. You might begin by duplicating the designs shown here and then strike out and create whatever effect you wish!

A design made of paper can always have new layers added, so that you are able to vary the effect until you find just exactly what pleases you. Or, with an inexpensive wall hanging like the paper sunflower, you can well afford to start over again.

Tissue Paper Sunflower

The paper sunflower picture (page 62) uses richly coloured tissue paper but effective results can be got from cartridge paper or even corrugated cardboard. A touch of whimsy like the emerald feather can always be added.

For this sunflower of tissue, cut out circles of tissue paper to the size and in the colour(s) desired for the finished flower, and fold into equal parts making a triangle, one side of which is curved (see left hand diagram, above). Cut triangular shapes (A) in the top to form petals and rounded shape (B) for the centre. Glue the centre to a board background. Add as many layers of circles as you wish. Curve the petal fringe forward into a cup shape and spray with clear lacquer. Add on a wool stem either by sticking or couching, or leaf of cut, folded green paper.

Crayon Crafts

Landmarks of different cities of the world provide the theme for these wall hangings. Crayon techniques have been used to create colourful pictures illustrating three major cities. First of all choose your subject. You can reproduce the illustrations on pages 64 and 65, or design your own by making sketches in an interesting city of characteristic buildings, scenes or people, then combine the sketches in a picture.

If you have decided to make a copy and the original sketch is not to scale, it is fairly easy to enlarge or reduce a particular illustration, photograph or greetings card which attracts you.

To obtain an enlargement, first draw a rectangle or square round the chosen material. Divide this into $\frac{1}{2}$ inch squares, carefully numbering the dividing lines and matching numbers at top and bottom and again on both sides. Draw another rectangle replacing each $\frac{1}{2}$ inch square with a 1 inch square, numbering the lines in exactly the same way as for the first rectangle. Watching carefully where the illustration crosses the construction in the first rectangle, reproduce the drawing in the larger rectangle. In this manner, the drawing is enlarged to twice its original size and it is easy to see that, by varying the size of the second rectangle, the original may be enlarged by a third, a quarter or as large as is desired. By reversing the process the original may be reduced; that is by placing the original sketch in a rectangle and dividing the rectangle into 1 inch squares which must be numbered as before. Draw another rectangle replacing each 1 inch square with $\frac{1}{2}$ inch squares matching the numbers of the larger squares. By repeating the process described above, an accurate reduction can be achieved.

The techniques for these three examples vary. The City of Istanbul uses a crayon overlay technique, Tokyo is done on crayoned scraper board, and Rome is a crayon transfergraph. The size of each is about 1 foot long by 4 inches wide.

Crayoned Scraper Board

The **City of Tokyo** (page 64, left) is done on scraper board. All the areas in the design are outlined in pencil on the scraper board and, when the design is satisfactory, the pencil lines are re-drawn in Indian ink with a wide nib pen. The width of the line is determined by the size and intricacy of the shape and the amount of detail required.

When the ink lines are dry, wax crayon is rubbed heavily in each shape. A thin coat of Indian ink or tempera paint is applied over the design. This can be brushed on easily by using soap on the brush occasionally while it is being painted, or it can be rubbed on with a soft cloth. The over-

coating is then scratched off with pointed tools such as pens, styli or combs.

Crayon transfergraph

The **City of Rome** (page 64, right) is done by the technique known as crayon transfergraph. The materials required are coloured chalks, wax crayons and drawing paper with enough texture to hold a firm application of chalk. Transfer can be used to achieve unique and delightful colour and texture effects. The colours needed for the composition are decided upon first, and then they are laid on the sheet of paper in the correct order for transfer to another paper.

To begin a transfergraph, apply coloured chalk rather heavily to a sheet of drawing paper. Next apply a layer of white waxed crayon over the chalk. Then add another layer of coloured wax crayon over the white layer. The colour of this last layer should be decided upon in your preliminary planning. Should a generally darker impression of the chalk be desired, the final colour can be black. However, you may achieve some surprising results when different wax crayon colours, as well as similar ones, are used in combination with almost any colour of chalk.

When the preparatory sheet is ready, place a sheet of poster paper, unprinted newspaper, typing or ledger paper on it. A sketch of the design can be drawn on the back of the smooth transfer sheet. Use a fairly hard pencil or stylus to draw or re-draw the design on the back of the sheet. This transfers colour to the smooth paper. Or, place the colour sheet face down on a smooth surface, then draw your design on back of the colour sheet. It is advisable to use this approach if lettering is part of the design.

Crayon Overlay

The **City of Istanbul** composition is first painted with smooth, flat tempera; this forms the background and small details need not be included in this under-painting. When the paint has dried, wax crayon is applied heavily all over the design.

Having applied the crayon overlay, begin scraping it off in varying degrees to reproduce the details of the original. You can use a table knife or nail file or other household tool for this. The tool that is used, the way it is used and the extent to which the wax crayon is removed, determines the colour, texture, detail and design of the picture.

Looking again at the wall hanging of the City of Rome, it is easy to see how the three original sketches on page 67 can be combined to make up an interesting and colourful transfergraph. Tracings of the sketches should be placed one on top of the other until you arrive at a satisfactory composition.

Sketching and Painting

Other techniques, not illustrated here, are equally interesting—the dramatic appeal of a charcoal drawing, the soft freshness of a water-colour, detail in a tempera painting or the bold statement of an oil painting.

A good cartridge paper pad and a charcoal pencil are all that is needed for a charcoal sketch. Charcoal sticks are messy and the drawing is apt to smudge and blur. Charcoal pencils are more manageable, but the finished sketch still needs to be sprayed with a fixative, which nowadays just means a small aerosol-type container with a spray.

Good water-colour paper, a selection of good sable paint brushes and a box of artists' water-colour paints should be indulged in before attempting water-colour sketches. Work should never be done in hot sunlight as the colour dries too quickly and loses its fluid character.

Tempera painting should really be executed on a gesso ground and for this medium, powder colour should be mixed with egg, size or milk. An under-coat of complementary colours is usually laid beneath the final colour scheme.

Oil paints, brushes, canvas, a palette and an easel are necessary equipment for oil painting. Flower studies, landscapes, portraits or interiors are all suitable subjects in this medium.

Any sketch of your own, however simple, has far more value than a copy of an illustration or photograph. Any copy is simply second-hand and a lazy way to work. A sketch book, selection of pencils and pens, and a box of crayons should be part of everyone's holiday equipment. A personal technique is soon developed by sketching the simplest things. The eye soon learns to see a decorative shape or an attractive composition. Following a feeling for shapes, comes a feeling for colour, and a wonderful selection of coloured crayons is available to satisfy this sensitivity. Confidence grows as the sketching progresses and an interest in balance, rhythm and proportion develops—all ingredients which must go into a good composition. The eye becomes more discerning and learns to exaggerate or eliminate various details and, with practice, a personal style begins to emerge which gives the work distinction and value.

Copper Creations

Copper foil is easy to handle; it can be cut with scissors and is more malleable than tin, so that it makes light and graceful Christmas decorations and reflects lighting. It is also fire-proof.

On page 69 you will see some designs made from copper foil. They can be hung as mobiles or

mounted on a panel as a wall hanging with a felt or flock paper backing.

The patterns should first be traced on the foil, using a blunt pencil. Cut out with scissors. The surface of the foil can be painted with transparent glass lacquers or opaque model aeroplane enamels and finally decorated with sequins and beads stuck on with transparent glue.

The diagram on page 68, bottom left, was first enlarged to the desired size and then used to transfer the design to copper foil to achieve the decoration (page 68, top left). The diagram was constructed with compasses by drawing three circles; the first uses a suitable radius for the centre shape of the finished decoration. With the same centre point and twice the first radius, a second circle was drawn, marking the edge of the fringed circle shown in the illustration. Again with the same centre point and three times the first radius, another circle was drawn to give the length of the eight spokes shown in the diagram, and angles of 45° marked off with a protractor at the same centre point as that of the circles to give the centre line of each spoke.

This diagram or template was then used to transfer the design to the copper foil. The shapes between the spokes and the inner circle were fringed and the centre circle textured by placing it face down on a soft surface and pressing with the point of a blunt pencil. Lines were cut into the centre on either side of the middle shape of each spoke and on the side shapes of each spoke.

The decorations illustrated on page 69 are made from copper foil and wire shapes, stuck together with clear Bostik.

Figure 1 is a simple circle of copper foil with four small concentric circles of wire in the centre, surrounded by a number of small seed-like shapes. It has a tail like a scroll and three smaller shapes, triangular in character, all decorated with small wire seed-like shapes.

Figure 2 has a large frilled circle with a smaller frilled circle superimposed on it. A flower shape with a small circle in the centre and small triangles between the petals is surrounded by a ring of dots. Wire loops are attached to the outer edge.

Figure 3 is made up of two square pieces of foil of the same size set crosswise on top of one another. Two frilled circular shapes, one slightly smaller than the other, are stuck on top again. There are three small concentric circles in the centre, surrounded by seed-like shapes arranged as petals tipped with small circles.

Figure 4 is divided by folding paper to make a template as described on page 68. Here the circle is divided into sixteen sections, with seed-like shapes added to them, surrounding two small wire concentric circles with a small spider shape in the centre.

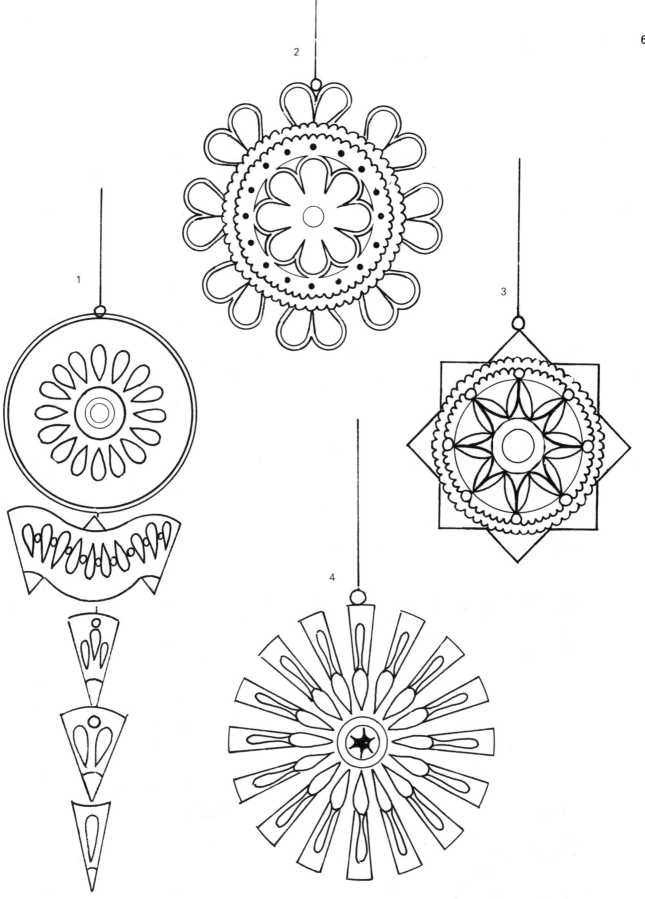

Silk Screen Printing

Silk screen printing is a simple process in which the design and background are painted on the screen in shellac leaving the shapes to be printed clear, so that the screen must be prepared for each colour in the design.

The pattern is printed on the required article, Christmas or invitation card, picture or illustration, by pulling ink of the desired colour down the framed, hinged screen with a rubber-edged tool called a squeegee. The process is repeated for each colour in the design, using the particular screen prepared for that colour. Silk is a very hard wearing material so that quite a few prints can be made and if the screens are cleaned carefully the colour scheme may be varied but not the number of colours in a design.

You first need a silk screen (page 70). This is basically a hinged wooden tray with its bottom replaced by a silk, nylon or steel mesh, and can be bought in a variety of sizes.

Lay a piece of cardboard beneath the screen to keep the wood base clean. Draw your design on a sheet of paper the size of the card or paper you are going to print and place it on the cardboard. Close the screen and adjust the paper until your design is centred. Register marks placed on the cardboard help you to line up the corners or sides of succeeding papers.

Apply shellac directly on to the screen leaving a small gap between the design and screen. Keep the design in position beneath the screen while tracing over it and stopping out the background. Practise first on paper to get the feel of the amount of shellac required on the brush. Though the shellac is thick it hardens quickly. Brace the frame open and allow to remain in this position for 30 minutes so that the shellac will set.

Repeat this process to strengthen the outline of the design and when it is completely dry, forming a stencil, pour ink along the upper side of the screen in a line above the pattern. Hold squeegee at a 45-degree angle inside the screen and with one stroke draw the solution down slowly and evenly. Repeat this ink treatment for each of the cards to be printed.

Screen printing on material is a similar process although a larger screen is normally used to allow the ground to be covered more quickly. Stretch organdie or silk very tightly over a frame and have the areas of colour clearly marked on the design. Place the design under the screen as before and leave a tiny gap so that the shellac does not stick the screen to the design. Block out all areas except the first colour you have decided to print. Prepare screens for each colour in this way unless the desired colour can be achieved by over-printing, i.e. blue over yellow which will give a green.

Various types of dyes for materials are available. Some need steaming to fix them and others need ironing or baking but they should all come with explicit instructions.

The material to be printed should be stretched on a flat table and marked to give some idea of where the screen is to be placed. This is usually done by extending threads across the stretched material. With the screen in position and firmly held, pour enough dye into the top of the screen to cover the area to be printed. This should then be drawn firmly across the screen using a squeegee. The process is repeated for every imprint of the design on the material until all of one colour is printed on to the material. Second and third colours follow, making sure all the shapes fit into position in the design.

The dye must not be allowed to dry in the screen which should be carefully washed as the printing is finished, in plenty of clean, warm water, if it is to be used again.

Moulded Plastic

The room divider (right) was moulded in two sizes of flat glass or disposable pans. Any small Pyrex dish, ash tray or bowl will make an excellent mould when using the new Liquid Plastic. No heating is necessary. A hardener is added to the plastic, plus colour pigment to give bright non-fading colours. White may be added to give a full range of tints. Mould Release Wax, Liquid Plastic and Hardener with full instructions are obtainable from your local stockist.

Hardener is well stirred into the Liquid Plastic and poured into the waxed mould to cover the base. The mould is left in a warm place, such as the plate rack of a cooker or in front of a gas or electric fire, on a level surface, and left to set until the plastic will not move when the mould is tilted. This will take 20 minutes to an hour, depending on the temperature of the room.

If any object is to be embedded (shells, butterflies, flowers, stamps, medals, cut-out shapes representing leaves, abstract shapes or strips in foil or paper), it should be placed face downwards on the top layer. A mixture of Liquid Plastic and Hardener should be well stirred and poured over the object to cover it completely. Again place the mould in a warm spot on a level surface and leave to set for an hour.

Colour pigment is added to the Liquid Plastic and Hardener for the third layer, poured over the second layer to cover it completely and left to dry until the plastic cannot be scraped away with a finger nail.

To remove the casting from the mould immerse it completely in very hot water for 10 minutes, transfer and immerse the mould plastic side down in very cold water for 10 minutes. Repeat these two operations and the cast will drop out of the mould.

The planning of any chains or hooks must be taken into consideration before the plastic is poured into the mould. Small pegs (pieces of matchsticks would do), placed on end in the mould and well-covered with Mould Release Wax, will leave a hole when they are removed after the casting is finally taken from the mould.

Designs in Cement

Pebbles polished smooth by the sea, starfish, sea shells and other oddments are embedded in free-flowing waves of tinted cement.

To create this sort of mural, work out exactly the lines of your design on tracing paper. Then make a second copy, using one pattern to arrange stones, shells and other objects until you have found the design you want. Frame a piece of fine wire netting with a wooden lath and, using the second pattern as a guide, cut lengths of aluminium strip the same depth as the cement is to be, and the same length as the flowing lines in the design. These must be tacked or stuck into position to make walls to keep the various colours of cement apart.

Pour in cement tinted with water paint following the lines of your design. Position stones and shells according to pattern while the cement is still wet.

The cement will make this decoration fairly heavy, so Rawlplugs will be necessary through the lath into the wall if it is to be hung.

Cement Painting

the frame by nailing lengths of wood around the edges of the plywood.

To make the cement for the background mix water with pre-mixed sand and concrete and fill the frame to a depth of about ¾ inch. Use an ordinary garden trowel to smooth the wet concrete and work it into the wire netting.

When the concrete is level and smooth but still wet, start forming the design. An old spoon, a piece of wood, or proper modelling tools can be used for this work. Rough out the design on

A firm framework for the wet concrete is the first essential for this method of 'painting', which is similar to a method of mural decoration used by the Egyptians and Italians. For the base, nail a piece of wire netting to a rectangle or square of ½ inch plywood exactly the size you want for the finished painting, exclusive of framing. Next add

paper first and use this as a guide when you start on the concrete. To vary the effect a few pebbles or shells could be embedded in the concrete.

After this is finished and the cement is dry you can begin to paint using artists' oil colours and stiff bristled brushes. If the paint is used sparingly on the background, a subtle effect can be achieved.

Modelling Shapes

The substance called modelling 'goop' is a mixture which you can make yourself. It is extremely versatile and clean to use. The mixture can be rolled, cut, moulded or woven into shape, left white with a smooth or rough surface, or alternatively, painted and varnished.

The recipe for the mixture itself is simple. To make 1¾ pounds, mix 2 cups of table salt and ⅔ cup of water in a saucepan and stir over heat for 3 or 4 minutes. Remove the pan from the heat and stir in 1 cup of cornflour mixed with ½ cup of cold water.

The mixture should be the consistency of stiff 'dough. If it is not, then replace over a low heat and stir until the desired consistency is reached.

The mixture can be left white or divided into portions and coloured with a variety of food dyes. Alternatively, the moulded objects may be decorated or painted once they are dry.

The mixture will keep indefinitely if it is well wrapped in clear plastic or tin foil. This is very useful as it means that it may be used again and again by children.

Objects may be shaped in the hands, or the mixture may be rolled out thinly so that it can be wrapped round a foam rubber or other core. Place finished objects on a wire rack or screen, so that air will move freely around the surfaces and allow an average of about 36 hours at room temperature for the objects to dry, depending on their thickness. Objects with a large mass of 'goop' should be pierced when moist to allow the interiors to dry.

The examples shown here include a **wall plaque** formed with squares of the dried mixture painted and coated with shellac, and pegged to fibre board.

The **white bird** is made of the mixture shaped around plastic foam. The legs and beak are made of wire and are fixed into position when the 'goop' is still wet. The rough texture suggesting feathers is added by lightly patting with a stiff brush before the mixture is dry.

it by the edges, and allow to dry flat. You may want to pull several prints to get the best effect from your original design.

Paper Mosaics

This colourful wall hanging is simply constructed using smooth-surfaced papers in assorted colours, for example, the samples of paint colours. Having outlined this design or one of your own in full size on paper, cut up paint samples or coloured paper in various angular shapes to fill in the outline, but not necessarily fitting precisely. The use of closely related colours gives the effect of shading and adds depth.

The background chosen for this example is a rectangle of thin plywood covered with wood-grained plastic which can be bought with adhesive backing (available in hardware shops). Alternatively, the plywood can be left uncovered and stained a suitable colour. Chip-board makes another suitable background and has a very interesting texture.

Having attached the plastic material to the plywood, glue the pieces of paper in position on the plastic with rubber cement. A narrow gilt frame completes this wall decoration which only needs two eyelets screwed at the same level in the back of the frame to attach it to the wall.

Block Printing

Block printing is a skilled craft but there are adaptations for the layman. One of the easiest of these is the method shown here, using plastic foam. The results are very satisfactory.

For this method, you need a sheet of plastic foam, a sharp knife, a water-base paint, a paint tray and roller and some heavy smooth paper, such as cartridge paper.

Choose a design with simple bold outlines and scale it to fit. Then lightly scratch the design on the sheet of plastic foam (a straight pin will do for this). After this, take a sharp serrated knife and outline the design with deep v-shaped cuts, ensuring that they do not go completely through the foam.

Roll water-base paint on the foam, covering it evenly, and then spread a sheet of heavy paper over the block and rub it gently with your hands, starting at the centre and working toward the edges.

Pull the paper carefully off the block, holding

Mosaics

Mosaics are an ancient art which today provide a simple means of making your own designs using bought mosaic tiles or natural materials like pebbles or seeds.

To make **seed mosaics** all that is required is a collection of oats, peas, beans, barley, coffee, spices and rice, plus tree bark, seedpods, bits of glass and a pot of glue.

The mosaic is done on a base of wood or thin plywood and should be reinforced with battens (narrow strips glued to the back) to prevent warping. Before using any natural materials it is necessary to sterilize them by heating at about 350°F for 15 minutes.

Outline your design on tracing paper, numbering and naming materials and colours to be used, and then retrace the design on the plywood. To fill in your design, work from the edges to the centre. Spread the main outlines with glue and set in larger seeds with tweezers. Spread glue fairly thickly over an area before sprinkling seeds over it rather more densely than required, since some inevitably fall off later. Press the seeds down well with a firm cloth pad.

The finished mosaic picture is best left flat for at least 36 hours and then sprayed with clear plastic or coated with polyurethane varnish. This will preserve the surface and make it both waterproof and heatproof. Each coat of varnish should be given 8 to 12 hours to dry.

For **tile mosaics**, the tiles come in porcelain, marble, ceramics and glass. The other materials you will require are a cutter, glue and grouting cement (all available at hardware shops).

Lay the tiles in the design you want on paper cut to size. Then transfer tiles one by one to the backing. To do this, apply a small dab of adhesive to the base itself or to the back of each tile. Press each tile firmly on the backing and allow the whole design to set overnight. Grouting is used to give a finish by filling the areas between tiles. Spread the mixture and press into the crevices. Allow the grouting 5 minutes to set before wiping off the excess, and then let the whole design stand for a few hours. Finally, wash it thoroughly with a sponge to clean it.

The complicated-looking table (top right) is really a simple design using the tile technique on a round base to which legs are attached.

The basis of the handsome ashtray (centre right) is a baking tin.

The materials you will require to make **pebble mosaic** panels (bottom right) are ready-mixed cement, a selection of different colours and textures of pebbles, and a wooden and mesh frame.

First make a wooden frame (or mould) measuring $12 \times 18 \times \frac{3}{4}$ inches. Form the corners with angle irons and set the frame unattached on a $13 \times 19 \times \frac{1}{4}$ inch base.

Saturate the inner wood areas of the frame with water. Trowel a base layer of cement into the frame a little at a time until it is $\frac{1}{4}$ inch deep. Press the cement down well, filling in the corners, and level off the surface with a trowel. Cut a piece of wire mesh to the exact inner measurement of the mould. Then, holding the mesh firmly with both hands, lay one edge (the front edge) against the frame and drop the mesh on to the cement. Press the mesh firmly down into the cement until it feels anchored there.

Now add a layer of cement on top of the wire mesh so that the cement is level with the frame top. Press this down and work into place. This top layer secures the mesh and holds the pebbles. Place a flat piece of wood stripping (about 4 inches longer than the frame) at the front of the mould and holding the ends with both hands work the wood rhythmically from side to side across the surface of the cement, working towards you. This is to smooth off the surface cement.

Pebbles collected from a beach or garden can be laid out in a design on paper the same size as the inner mould. When you have decided on the composition of the mosaic, lay the pebbles in place on the cement one at a time. Anchor each by holding it firmly and wriggling it into position.

Then, using a trowel or small rubber mallet, pound each pebble deep enough into the cement to be held firmly there. Allow at least 24 hours for the mosaic to set. When it has set, hold the mosaic upright and gently tap the frame around the edges and on the edge of the base to release the cement. The mosaic should come away from the frame quite easily.

When all the panels required have been completed you can apply waterproof tile mastic to the back of the mosaic and to the area to be covered by the mosaic. When the mastic gets tacky, place the mosaic panels in position to form an attractive garden decoration.

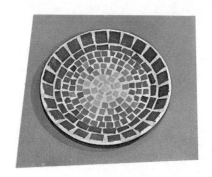

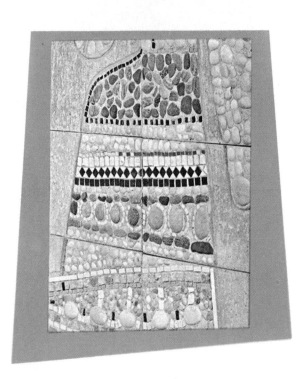

For Children

A child's interest in collecting things can be encouraged and made more enjoyable by making it possible for him to organize and display his collection.

Display panels to which a child might like to glue objects can be painted and hung in a bedroom. Older children might be more interested in collecting things which they can use: ferns dried and mounted decorate a placemat, flowers embedded in moulded plastic make paperweights.

Fibre board can be painted different colours for different collections, and objects pinned to it are easily removed again if necessary, accommodating a child's tendency to bring home the new things that attract his attention, shells, rocks, leaves, etc. Ideas for displaying prized objects might be to show everything of one colour together—shells, butterflies, seeds and flowers, for example, or to identify and classify objects separately—wild flowers, feathers, leaves, insects, butterflies and moths.

For the younger members of the family—and you will find you enjoy helping them—simple handicrafts are great fun. Stamping designs on notepaper or gift wrapping, or cutting birds and animals from paper help to pass a rainy day.

Potato printing, by the method shown (page 78), is just as satisfying as finger painting and far less messy. To make designs on potatoes, first draw the outline, then cut away the unneeded areas, leaving only the raised printing surface. Cover the surface with paint by dipping in a saucer of poster colour or finger paint, and stamp it on notepaper, gift wrapping, or accessories such as scarves or belts.

Attractive table mats can be made in this way, too, but for printing on material fabric printing dyes should be used. These are obtainable with full instructions. The potato block should be pressed on to a pad of material or a piece of felt saturated in the dye. In this way the amount of

dye picked up on the pad is limited and the edges of shapes are less blurred as a result.

The designs can take any form (stars, birds, stylized trees or fruit, for example).

A flock of **paper birds** cut from light cartridge paper makes a simple decoration that is fun for all the family. The bodies are in one piece, the wings another.

Using the pattern given below, cut wings and

bird's body from one sheet of paper. Fold the wings across the centre and glue to the body. Birds can be left as they are and a wire attached (see diagram) for hanging on a Christmas tree or they can be painted in bright colours or patterns complementing the child's bedroom scheme.

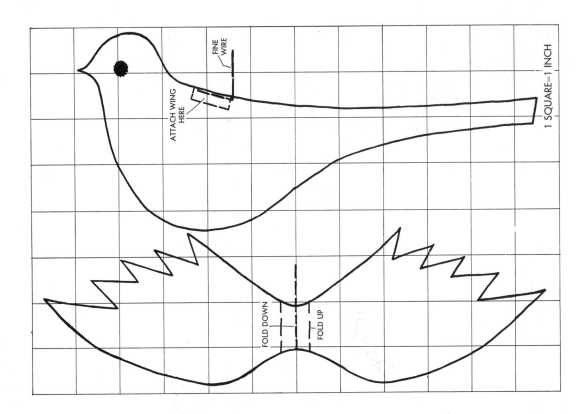

FINE WIRE

ATTACH WING HERE

1 SQUARE = 1 INCH

FOLD DOWN

FOLD UP

Rope Toys and Crafts

Another technique which will appeal to children is used to make the hairy lion on the left, using rope, hemp, twine and felt.

The method is quite simple and can be used for all sorts of creatures. Unwind one strand of each length of rope and insert two lengths of florist's wire. Then wind the strand, together with the wire, back into place. This stiffens the rope and enables the animal to stand.

For Christmas, children might find it fun to use the same method for a manger scene.

Rope Lion

For the rope lion you will need 12 inches of $1\frac{1}{2}$ inch rope, 24 inches of $\frac{1}{2}$ inch rope, 10 inches of $\frac{3}{8}$ inch rope, 2 yards of Manilla twine, scraps of green and red felt, and six pieces of 18 inch long florist's wire.

To make the legs, cut the 24 inch piece of rope into two 12 inch lengths and then wire each piece. Tie the ends with a small length of florist's wire and fray to make the feet.

Lay the two leg pieces flat. Add the $1\frac{1}{2}$ inch rope and the $\frac{3}{8}$ inch rope. Wrap the two body pieces together with the Manilla twine for about 1 inch. Add in the leg pieces, continue winding for about 3 more inches and fasten the twine with a knot. There will then be about 8 inches of rope left for the neck and head. Unwind the three strands and follow the instructions in the diagram below to make the head. Finally the rope ends are frayed to form the mane.

When adding wire to the rope, be sure to use the same length of wire as rope. Replace the strand over the wire and then wire or glue the rope into place.

This method of making rope toys can be adapted to make numerous other animals—horses, deer, cats, dogs, giraffes.

The success of these toys depends on interpreting the main characteristics of each animal and this depends largely on the proportions of the species.

When studying figure drawing in a life class students are taught that the proportions are based on the number of times the length of the head can be divided into the length of the trunk, legs and arms. Animals can be studied in the same way, so that by looking carefully at a photograph of a giraffe—or paying a visit to the zoo—the length of its neck can be determined by measuring how many times the length of its head can be divided into the length of its neck. In the same way the length of the fore legs, hind legs and body can be gauged. When the correct proportions are decided, a characteristic pose must be chosen and a sketch made on an appropriate scale which will keep this pose in mind. Then, using the same technique as for the lion, another creature can be evolved.

Domestic pets will make the easiest and most obliging models to enlist and for those youngsters lucky enough to have rabbits, tortoises, hamsters, frogs, ducks or chickens there is considerable raw material for design experiments.

An ambitious child could attempt pairs of animals about to enter the ark. A subject on this scale offers endless possibilities and hours of happy enjoyment on wet afternoons, and also, of course, helps to develop the imagination.

At Christmas time a manger scene could be attempted incorporating human as well as animal subjects. The rope figures would blend well with a wooden manger and straw.

This craft has been developed in Spain on a large scale as part of the tourist trade and has a lot in common with our own country art of plaiting corn dollies. In Spain also it was originally probably a country craft but it is now being exploited in all the favourite coastal resorts on the Costa Brava.

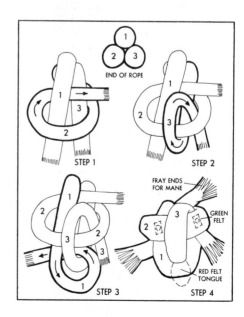

Circus Toys to Make

Circus Toys to Make

For children and adults who enjoy making toys here are some basic instructions (pages 82–5) that can be adapted to make all sorts of animals. You use whatever materials are at hand; boxes, cores from wax paper or tin foil, clear plastic wrapping and remnants of fabrics are some suggestions. You will also need glue and a variety of papers and trimmings.

The **giraffe** has a toothpaste box body; the front leg and neck are made from a 12 inch core from a role of tin foil. Slip the core into holes in the toothpaste box; the longer one goes through the front and back of the toothpaste box to form the front leg and neck. A shorter core, forming the back leg, fits into a hole cut in the underside of the box.

A small box forms the head. Cut a circle in the underside of the box and fit the neck into it. This basic method can be used for any animal shape. It is best to assemble all the parts and then, when you are satisfied with the shape, take it apart again and cover the parts with fabric or paper, or paint the surfaces. Then reassemble the animal using paper fasteners inserted through both

sides of the body into the hollow cores (the heads of the fasteners are covered with black fabric pieces) and glue to attach the head. Wire loops form the ears and horns for the giraffe; they are put between pieces of textured fabric, glued or sewn together, then glued into slits made in the top of the head. The nose and hoofs are black fabric glued in place and the tail is made of unravelled cord.

The **clown** (page 83, top) is made from a box which forms its body, topped by a typewriter ribbon box for its hat. Use adhesive-backed paper to cover the box (here in black) and also for the facial features and hair. The ears are made of paper and glued to the sides of the box. A wire inserted into the hat is held inside by tape and an artificial daisy is added. The hat trimming is a cardboard circle between two pieces of adhesive paper, the edges of which are scalloped.

The **fuzzy-faced lion** (below) is a cut-off salt box $3\frac{1}{2}$ inches long. The open end is covered by a circular piece of cardboard. The core of a tin foil roll is inserted into a circular hole cut in the box and extends $1\frac{1}{2}$ inches below to hold the body up. The $4\frac{5}{8}$ inch long cores form the legs and paws (crush them slightly to form an oval shape). When you have assembled the parts, dismantle them and cover with textured fabric in yellows and browns. The legs are attached (level with the body at the back) to the core extended below the body with paper fasteners.

The ears are wire bent into shape and covered with fabric, then glued into place. The face is encircled with a fringe made from trimming and glued in place to form the mane; the whiskers are pipe cleaners and the eyes, nose, mouth and toes are coloured fabric cut from remnants and sewn or glued on.

The **llama** is attractive and easy to make, the body is a salt box covered with coloured paper. Legs, neck and head are made of cardboard (shoe-box cardboard is useful for this) covered in the same way and inserted into the slits made in the body box with a sharp knife. Twist a piece of coloured paper tightly to make the tail. Yellow spots, eyes, and the blanket fringe and decoration are poster paint, while the blanket itself is made from cartridge paper.

The **red lion** (page 85, top) has a small-size salt or spice box body and a lid for its head. Cover the body and head with coloured paper and then glue a disc of coloured paper over the end of the body. The tail is paper rolled tightly and glued, with cotton tipped orange sticks (available at any chemist's) inserted in the tail. These may be dipped in poster paint to give contrast colour at the tips.

For the face cover the lid with coloured paper, making sure you cover the raw edges (a strip of paper covers the rim and discs of paper can be used to cover the front and back).

The details on the face are made of coloured paper shapes glued in place and the stylized mane consists of orange sticks dipped in paint and inserted at various levels.

The fanciful **blue fuzzy elephant** (page 85, foot) has a powder or salt box covered in blue fabric as a body, and the bottom half of a typewriter ribbon box as a head. The trunk is formed by cutting two large pieces of fabric shaped to fit the head at the top, elongated into a trunk at the bottom.

Make one of these pieces the top piece, that is, the portion with eyes attached. The eyes are made by attaching small black circles of felt to larger white circles with small Straight stitches. The whites of the eyes are then sewn in position on the head, adding the eyebrows, which are small lengths of pipecleaner dipped into red paint and glued above each eye. The two pieces of the trunk are glued together, sandwiching a piece of wire down the centre from the top of the head to the end of the trunk. When dry, the top of the head-trunk piece is glued around the top of the typewriter ribbon box, letting the material fold over the centre wire so that the forehead protrudes outward. The ribbon container top is then slipped over the bottom section and glued. Pipe cleaner tusks should be made by poking a hole through each side of the head boxes so that a curved pipe cleaner can be slipped into position.

The saddle and harness are cut from scarlet felt and decorated with tiny brass buttons or sequins. The saddle has a leather fringe at both ends. Small scalloped pieces of white felt are attached to the front of each foot to suggest toes.

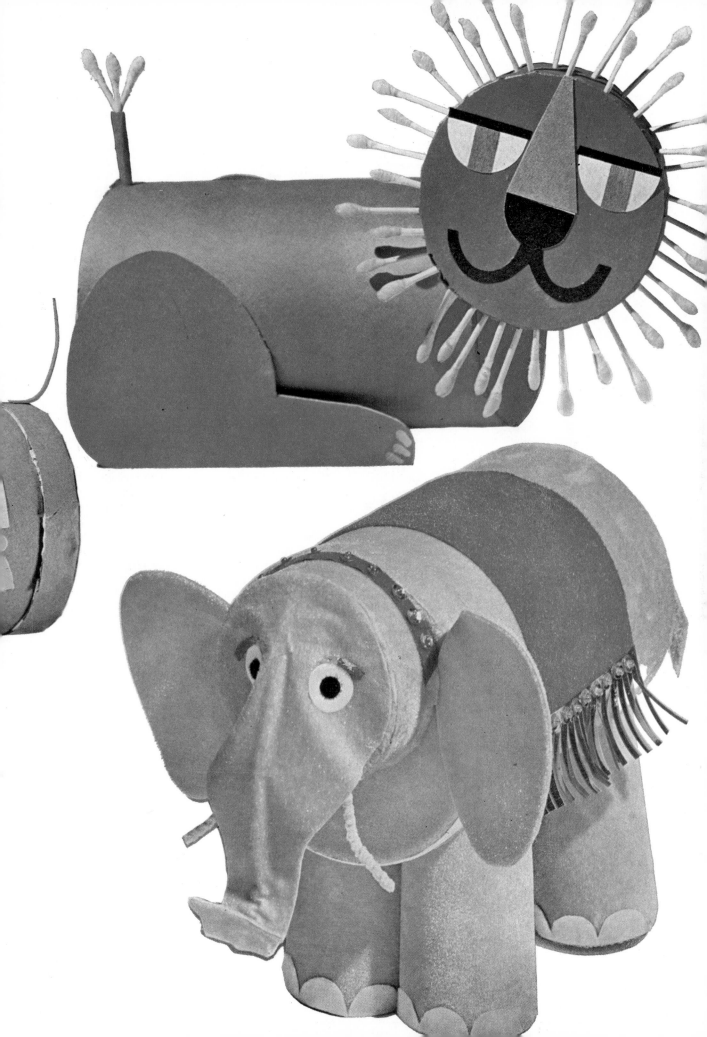

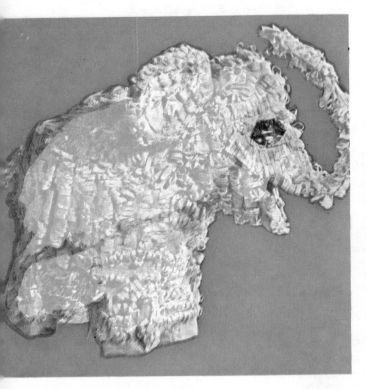

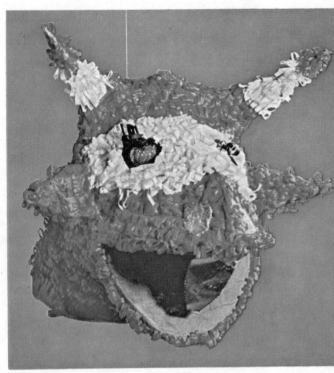

Pinatas

Mexicans, instead of hanging gifts from the Christmas tree, fill a *pinata* with small gifts or sweets, suspend it from the ceiling and allow the children to take turns at trying to hit it with a stick. The child who does so and breaks the *pinata* is the lucky one who gets the contents.

This is part of a nine day celebration before Christmas called *Los Posadas* when families meet to celebrate *posadas* which are a re-enacting of the Holy Family's search for lodging. They form processions and walk to a different house each night, where by singing they beg to be asked inside. This is refused at first but eventually they are admitted to kneel before the *Nacimiento* or nativity scene to pray. Then the celebrations can begin, dancing, eating and, finally, breaking the *pinatas*.

When making a *pinata*, be sure to make it

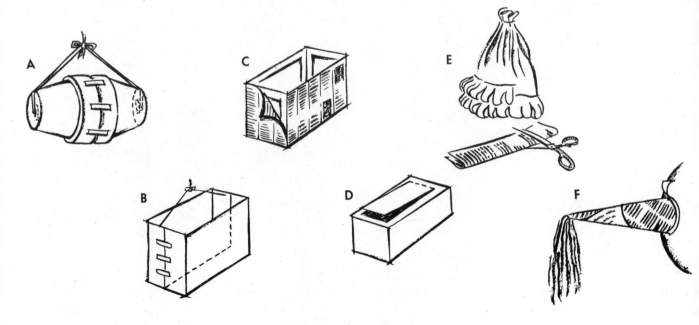

large enough to hold lots of little gifts and sweets and firm enough to be hung up, yet fragile enough to shatter with two or three blows. Mexican *pinatas* are formed around *ollas*, thin, round clay pots, which shatter easily.

Since these are not available in this country, one idea for making a pinata is to use two flowerpots taped together (see page 86, Figure A). To hang them, lace string tied to a narrow stick through the holes in the bases of the pots and hang them from a beam well clear of walls and decorations. With one firm blow the tapes should break and the contents come cascading down. But the pots may shatter too, so don't let anyone stand directly under them.

Alternatively, make *pinatas* from cardboard boxes (of shoe-box weight, for example). Cut a box in half lengthways (as shown in B and C, opposite) and tape it, or cut out the centres of the sides and cover with two thicknesses of newspaper. Another method is to cut out a flap from the bottom of a box (as shown in D, opposite) and achieve a trap-door effect.

Large paper bags also make good *pinatas* (as in E). Cover the bag by folding tissue or crêpe paper in half and putting fringes at the base. Use

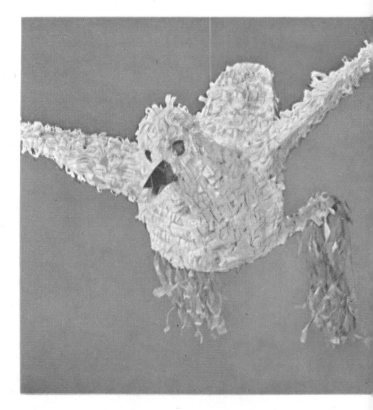

newspaper too for shapes such as the cone shape (in F) of the bull's ears.

The outside of these *pinatas* is made of rows of differently fringed coloured tissue or other very soft paper glued in strips around the basic shape.

The brightly coloured clown is a typical Mexican *pinata*. It and these other animals, the fierce red and white bull which has a gleaming gold tongue, the white dove with its blue streamers and the cheery pink elephant, will delight children with their vivid colours and imaginative shapes as well as with their contents.

These basic shapes are made from papier mâché the basis of which is paper. Old newspapers are the usual source of material and these are torn into scraps and boiled until they disintegrate. Add ½ teaspoon of oil of wintergreen to keep the mash smelling sweet and to prevent the growth of moulds and fungi. The mixture should be beaten with a whisk or electric beater until it is smooth.

Drain in a wire strainer or colander leaving the mash moist. Add 4 cups of flour to each gallon of mixture to absorb the moisture and make a paste. Re-heat the mixture with an asbestos mat under the saucepan as the flour scorches easily. Cook at a low temperature keeping the mixture covered for the first hour until the mash is thoroughly warm, then remove the saucepan lid and continue cooking until the mixture will stand in heaps by itself. When it is cool it is ready to model into any desired shape.

Games to Make

Simple indoor games are fun to make at home and fun to play.

A **billiard table** (below), cut from hardboard or plywood and covered with a fabric such as green felt, has holes into which shallow tins are placed to form the pockets. The table can be used on top of a card table. To make cues wooden dowels are used and the balls are made of plastic foam painted or sprayed the required colours, white, red, yellow, green, brown, blue, pink and black.

This is true too of **living room golf** (page 89).

To make the holes, cover tins with coloured paper and number them (using numbers cut from old calendars, for example) by glueing strips of shaped cardboard to the end of each tin as shown. The balls are again made of plastic foam as are the heads of the clubs. The club handles are wooden dowels.

Puppets and marionettes are fun, and easy for children to make. For the **puppets** cut out two outline shapes of the figure in coloured felt or any other fabric with body. Sew or glue these together leaving holes for four fingers and for the thumb. Add stuffing to the head and sew or glue on a face, using buttons for eyes, white curly wool for a beard, pieces of fabric for the mouth. Puppets can be placed in a setting, this enamelled box iced with Alabastine (top, right), for example.

The **marionettes** (centre, right) are made from inch plastic foam balls. Cut these in half and line the interior with felt for the hinge. Attach this to strings at the top and bottom (to allow the hinge to open and close). Pipe cleaners form legs and buttons or sweets are used for eyes (glued or sewn on). The television stage is made from a box with the front cut out, and lined with dark velvet.

A cardboard box (painted or else covered with coloured paper) as a base, and a tin foil roll core topped with a fabric or paper face go to make up the **poles for tossing rings** (bottom, right). The rings can be made from coloured fabric rolled firmly into a tube and then the two ends sewn together to form a circle. Decorate with stripes of different colours.

Another idea to amuse children is the **cardboard box target** any size will do) in which holes are cut large enough to admit the plastic foam balls. Assign numbers to the holes and decorate the box with bright colours and stripes. A returning device for the balls can be made by cutting 6 or 8 inches from the front panel of the box, then glueing a piece of cardboard at an angle on the inside.

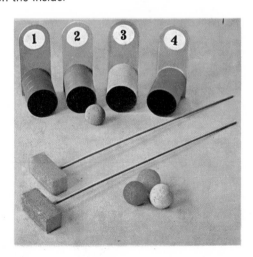

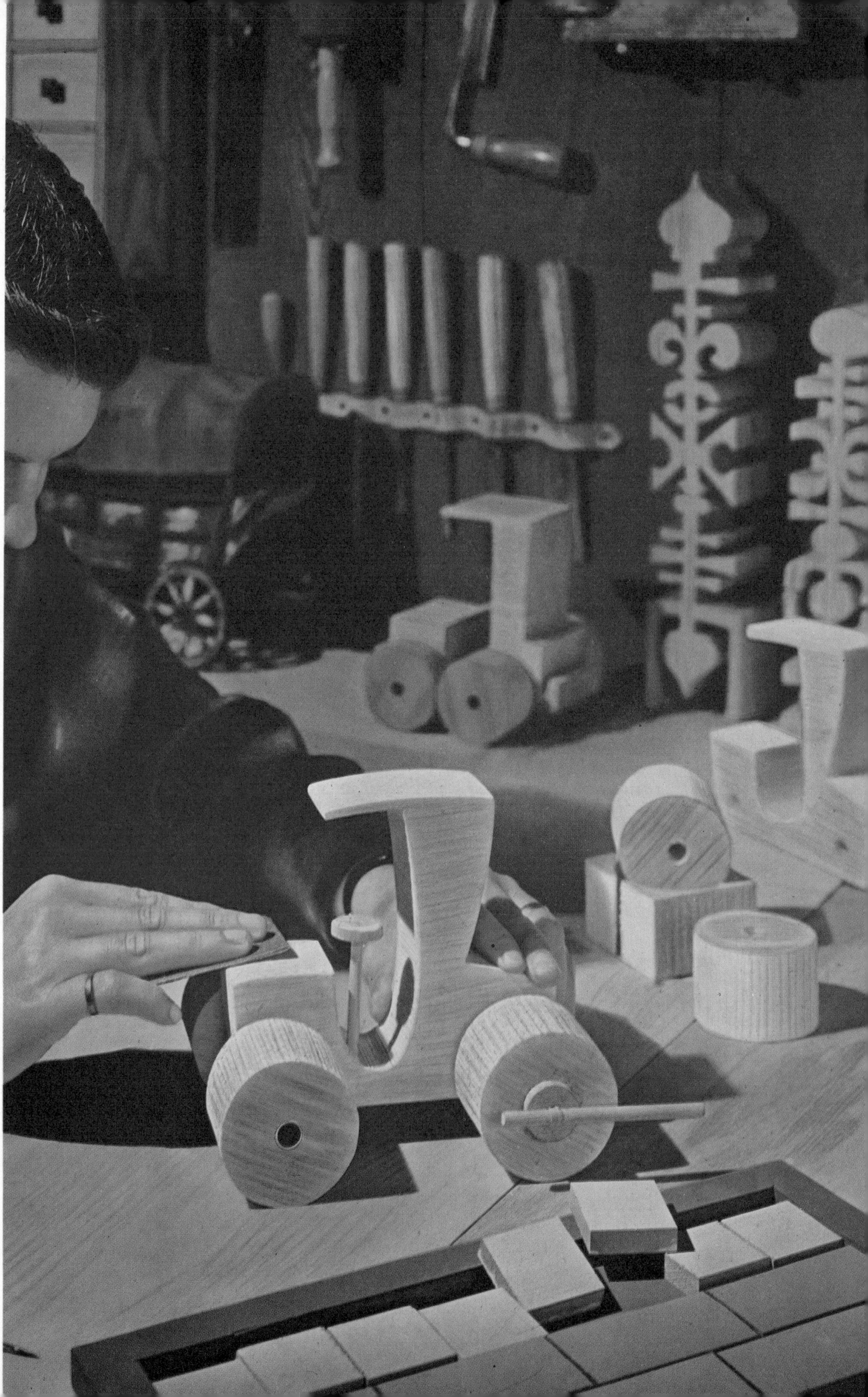

Working in Wood

Working with wood is a skilled craft about which amateurs can learn a lot. The material is low in cost and a process of trial and error produces some interesting results whether one is making toys or wall decorations.

Nursery Cars

Blocks of wood are used to make the little wooden cars (opposite) which are safe and uncomplicated toys ideal for any child. They are propelled on the spool and rubber band principle. Two inch blocks of wood (here white pine) are shaped with a jig saw attachment for the normal electric drill. The bodies are one solid piece of wood, with holes into which metal tubing axles are pushed and holes

for $\frac{1}{8}$ inch dowel (i.e. a wooden peg or plug) steering rods. A slice of $\frac{3}{4}$ inch dowel forms the steering wheel for each of the cars.

Metal tubing is pushed into the wheels and through the body to make the axles. For best effect the holes in the body should be drilled slightly larger in diameter than those in the wheels.

For a rear-wheel motor, wind a large rubber band around a 3 inch length of $\frac{1}{8}$ inch dowel. Draw the band through a small round dowel (which serves as a hub), then through the axle, and secure to a small nail on the opposite wheel. Then lubricate the hub with soap. After you have done this, wind the stick several times to start the car moving.

Finish the cars off by sanding the wood or, if you wish, sand and then paint each one several colours, using non-toxic paint.

Driftwood Designs

One slightly more unusual way of using wood is by making sand castings of interestingly shaped driftwood to be found on coasts and river banks across the country. Older children, as well as fathers, will enjoy creating these natural collage decorations.

To make a casting, smooth damp sand on a sand table as shown, banking it up around a piece of

driftwood to form the outline of a mould. Arrange the pieces of wood and vary the texture of the sand around them with a trowel. Then mix sand, water and casting plaster, and pour it over the wood and the background.

While the plaster is still moist add shells, pebbles, a sprinkling of coarse sand or other decorative details.

The finished casting may be mounted on hardboard for hanging.

Playroom Gifts

Gay and useful presents for the younger members of the family which will be fun to make.

Playhouse

The playhouse (below) is made from six 48 inch pieces of marine plywood (three 4 × 8 foot sheets are cut in half). Each of the square panels has two $\frac{1}{2}$ inch slots cut 4 inches in from each side halfway down each panel. Each panel

interlocks with the next at right angles. For entry, a 30 inch diameter hole is cut in the front and back panels.

A roof piece, made from a 1 inch × 4 inch piece joined to a 1 × 2 inch piece, is placed at the point where the two roof panels meet. All surfaces must be covered with an undercoat before the final bright colours are added. Simple designs can be stencilled on the panels with paint.

Sewing Table

For the sewing table, have the timber merchant cut two 24 inch circles from plywood. From the centre of these, cut 20 inch circles. You will have two 24 inch circles 4 inches wide. Glue these pieces together; clamp and let them dry overnight. Ready made wooden legs with metal tips are obtainable in craft shops. Double ended screws are inserted ready to install the legs in their correct position. Use either three or four. Paint the table in a bright colour. Glue a 2 inch piece of plastic on the outside circumference of the table.

The basket frame is made from strong cane. This is soaked to make it pliable, then woven into a spider to form the base and into a rim at the top to fit the 20 inch circle cut in the table top. Cut strips of felt to weave between the cane uprights of the basket. Place the basket in the centre of the table top.

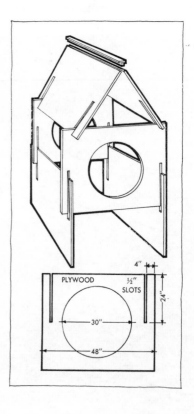

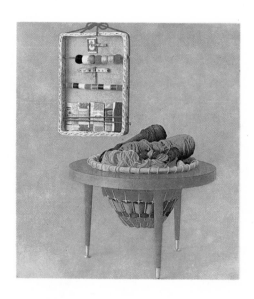

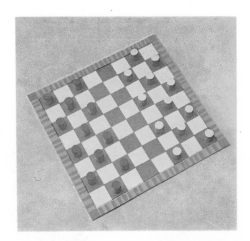

Draft Board

The draft board is colourful as well as handy to have at games time. It is made from painted plywood. Tissue paper squares in contrasting colours are applied with clear plastic spray or varnish. Any colour combination you wish can work effectively. This red and yellow scheme is a gay choice. Or, use a traditional red or white and black colour combination.

The drafts are easy to make. They are cut from 1 inch dowels and are sanded smooth. Coloured paper is glued on the tops. Varnish is added last.

Animal Nursery Benches

Amiable animals, a tiger and an elephant, make delightful benches for a tot's room. To duplicate these animals, have the timber merchant cut rectangles for bodies and round or square heads. Cut out rectangles from the sides to shape the four legs. Nail the five sides of the body together and nail on the head. Sand all edges until they are smooth.

Paint the animal a bright colour. Then, using a small brush for detailed work, paint on eyes, ears and other finishing touches. Or you can use bright designs cut from felt and glue them on. Bobble fringe makes an attractive trimming.

Pedestal Stands

Three handsome pedestal stands for junior collectors' pieces are salvaged from old oak newel posts. To adapt this idea for a playroom or other use, cut the posts to the height you desire and glue and nail on the square top platforms. Trim with wooden knobs at each corner. Sand and repaint in brilliant hues; or, stain if the wood grain is interesting.

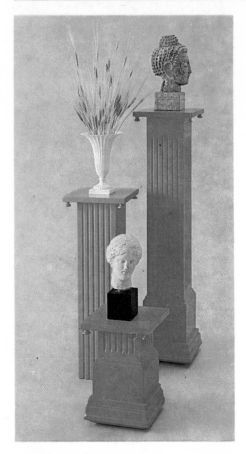

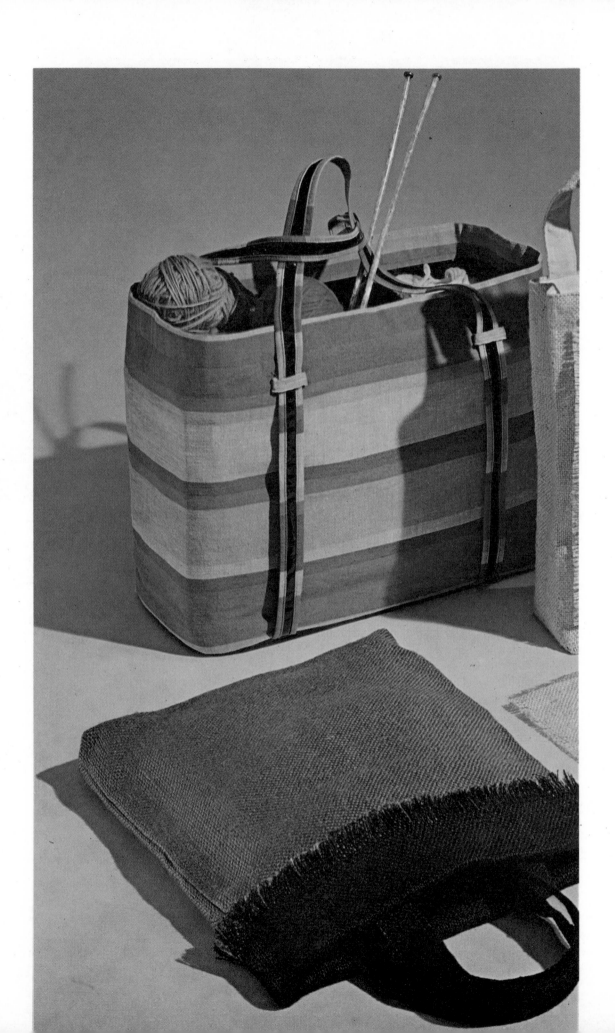

Holdalls

The brown and black **hessian bag** (lying down, page 94) is easy to make. Cut two pieces of hessian, one brown and one black, each 36 × 12 inches. With right side inside fold both pieces of material in half so that you have two shapes each 18 × 12 inches with a fold along one edge. Seam both pieces on both sides on the wrong side of the material from the fold to the open end, making two open-ended pockets. Turn brown shape to the right side and slip black shape inside it. Fringe the open ends and turn over for two inches so that the finished bag will be 16 × 12 inches.

Cut two pieces of black hessian 12 × 3 inches for the handles. Make $\frac{1}{4}$ inch turnings at either edge of strap and tack, then top-stitch along the length of both sides and attach to bag so that stitching is hidden beneath fringe.

The gay **striped bag** (page 94, top) is plastic lined so that it can double as a beach holdall in summer. Materials required are plastic curtain material for lining, furnished weight textured linen, cotton or towelling for the outside, black oilcloth for base and strap details, and heavy cardboard for base. Cut out materials according to pattern below.

Place cardboard (2) between two pieces of plastic (1), and stitch round edges. Join short sides of lining together, then outer fabric (3). Mark strap positions on lower edge of outer fabric $6\frac{1}{4}$ and $14\frac{1}{2}$ inches from side seam, then mark strap loop positions $4\frac{1}{4}$ inches from top edge and $6\frac{1}{4}$ and $14\frac{1}{4}$ inches from side seam.

For straps, place oilcloth strips (5) on centre of fabric strips (4), turn in raw edges of fabric leaving about $\frac{1}{4}$ inch each side, machine-stitch in position. For loops (6), fold material lengthwise across a third of its width and press; fold other edge on line reached by first edge, press and then fold in half again; stitch along centre of remaining width. Cut strips into four equal pieces, double ends under so that folded loop measures approximately $1\frac{1}{2}$ inches, stitch firmly in position. Thread straps through loops leaving raw ends at base of bag.

Turn outer material inside out, pin right edge of lining to seam allowance of base. Turn base over and with wrong side of fabric facing pin right lower edge to base. Seam allowance for base is now between right side edges of lining and fabric; push strap ends through at marks and pin. Stitch through all layers as close to cardboard as possible. Finish by turning outer side of fabric right out and stretch bag and straps until both lie smooth; stitch straps through bag fabric at back of loops. Neaten fabric and lining, then pin over the lining and turn in raw edge 1 inch, pin on inside, and machine-stitch from outside. Remove pins and press this seam. To avoid raw edges on inside of bag, make lining separately and once bag is right side out slide lining into position concealing seams. Turn in top edges and slip-stitch together.

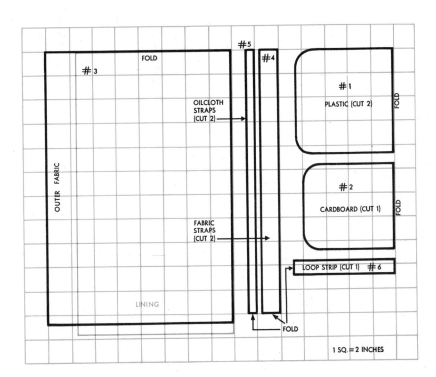

1 SQ. = 2 INCHES

Placemats

Place settings such as these for everyday and for picnics make attractive gifts. The examples here use very simple techniques.

Everyday Placemats

The **rose appliqué place setting** requires $\frac{1}{2}$ yard of white organdie and $\frac{1}{4}$ yard pink glazed cotton for 1 mat and 1 napkin.

For the placemat cut a piece of organdie 14 inches × 18 inches and a piece of cotton 6 inches square. Trace the rose design (from a gardening catalogue) on to the cotton, cut it out and place it on the organdie. Appliqué the outside edge of the rose in the placemat corner, 2 inches in from the side and lower edges, using Buttonhole stitch or machine set for a narrow zigzag. With white cotton thread, straight-stitch the lines inside the rose from the right side, and pull the ends to the wrong side and tie off.

The edge facings are made from a strip of the pink cotton, $1\frac{1}{2}$ inches wide, stitched to the edge from the wrong side. The corners are mitred by folding the surplus material away on each corner at an angle of 45° and concealing it within the hem, when it is being stitched flat on the right side with a $\frac{1}{4}$ inch turning.

To match the placemats cut napkins of organdie 12 × 12 inches in size and apply the facing of cotton as on the placemat.

For the **blue and white place settings** the material required is $1\frac{1}{2}$ yards of white linen and 2 yards of blue, plus stiff lining and contrasting thread for 2 mats and napkins.

Cut the mats and lining the same size, 18 inches × 14 inches. Select a decorative stitch, place organdie under the area to be decorated and stitch in contrasting thread. Sew the lining to the place-mat right sides together leaving one side open, turn to the right side and slip-stitch that edge.

Using the same method, make napkins in white linen 13 inches square and embroider the same stitch in blue.

The **gold place settings** (page 97, bottom) require $1\frac{1}{2}$ yards of linen and 14 yards of rickrack for four settings. The size of the mats is 18 inches × 12 inches and the napkins 14 inches square.

Stitch the rickrack on the right side of the mats and napkins, sewing through the centre of the trim. Fold and press; top-stitch to finish.

The set of **yellow placemats** (page 97, top) need $1\frac{1}{2}$ yards of linen and 7 yards of braid. Cut the mats 18 × 12 inches, the napkins 14 inches square. Braid is placed at the edges and sewn on, starting a few inches from the corner, and the edges of the mat are folded back from the stitching line to allow the braid to extend beyond the edges. Top-stitch close to the fabric fold. To finish off the napkin handroll the edges.

Some of the 'hand' methods of embroidery are more time-consuming but definitely more worthwhile. A hem-stitched hem with some drawn thread work within it has a very decorative effect and is perhaps all that is necessary by way of decoration.

Picnic Placemats

A rough-weave brightly striped material is used for these colourful and inexpensive place settings.

Cut the fabric to the desired size of placemat and bind the edges with a soft cotton trimming to tone with one of the stripes in the fabric.

Ties made from black ribbon are sewn to the back of one end of the mat; squares of the striped fabric give the ends of the ties a finished look.

If you wish, stitch two strips of the same colour fabric as the mat binding to make a holder for cutlery. When using the mats for picnics or barbecues, the cutlery can be placed in the pockets and rolled up so that guests can pick up both mats and cutlery at once. This is especially useful when serving a buffet meal.

Napkins in the same bold striped fabric are also an attractive addition to the table and should be given jaunty ties to match the mats.

Plain material with either matching or contrasting binding would be equally effective, but needs, perhaps, to be a fairly heavy fabric such as hessian or coarse linen to have that out-door feeling. Plastic would be less sophisticated but definitely more labour-saving as a wipe with a damp cloth would be enough to keep it fresh and clean.

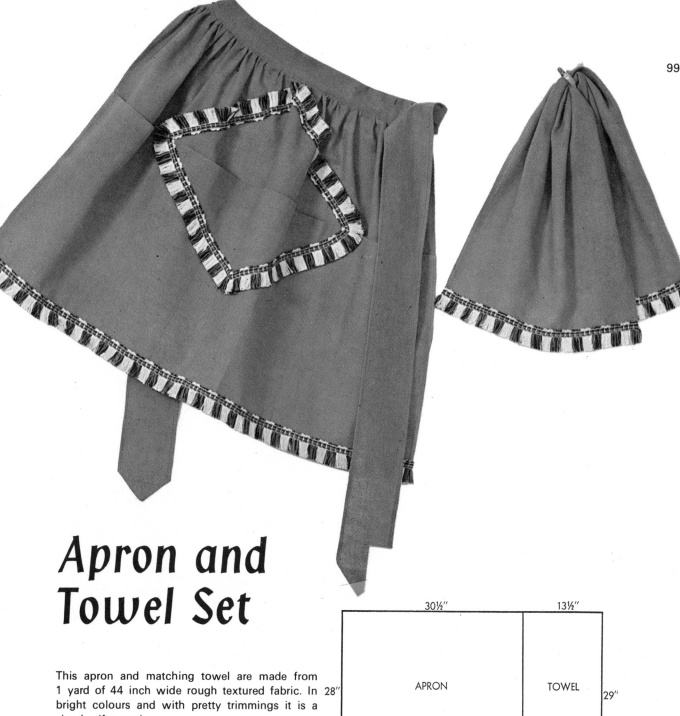

Apron and Towel Set

This apron and matching towel are made from 1 yard of 44 inch wide rough textured fabric. In bright colours and with pretty trimmings it is a simple gift to make.

Following the pattern given cut a 30½ × 28 inch long rectangle from 44 inch wide material. Make narrow hems at the sides and bottom. Fold up the length of the fabric 5 inches to form a long pocket 7 inches from the top of the apron and running the width of the apron. Top-stitch the fold in place at each side.

A multicoloured fringe is top-stitched to the apron in a diamond shape in the centre and this divides the pocket into three. The trimming is also stitched to the lower hemline. The top of the apron is gathered into a waistband 16 inches × 4 inches. Apron ties 4 inches × 28 inches in size are cut and the edges hemmed. Fold over the waist-

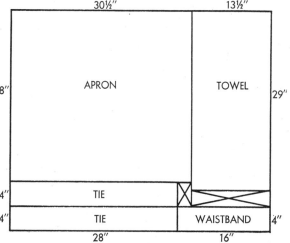

band and stitch it in place, catching in the ties as you do so.

The towel is cut 29 inches × 13½ inches in size and the hems turned. A trimming to match that on the apron is added to the towel ends.

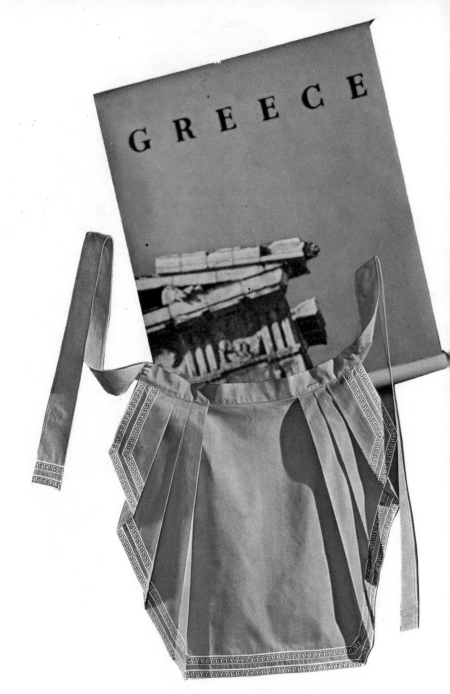

Aprons for Gifts

The pleated **Greek key apron** is made in cotton of a terracotta colour ($\frac{3}{4}$ yard of 36 inch wide is required) and is cut to include the soft pleats at the sides.

Make a waistband 4 × 16 inches, with two ties, each $1\frac{3}{4}$ × 30 inches in size. Fold apron material in half and cut off corners, then edge the border with two rows of the black and white Greek key trimming, which can be bought at haberdashery counters, hemming the edges of the apron at the same time. Tack the pleats at the top edge and then stitch the waistband on, stitching on the ties at the same time. Thus the whole top is stitched at once.

The **Japanese apron** has slit-openings giving this ivory-coloured apron an oriental touch. Cut the material as shown in the diagram (page 101, foot). Hem the ties and tops of pockets. Make darts in the top section. Top-stitch pockets into position an inch below the top edge of the lower section. Top-stitch lower section to top section centring carefully. Sew flat, red bias tape around sides, bottom and slit-openings. Attach ties to the waistband and stitch to the top of the apron. Slip-stitch frog closings to the pockets.

The **Scandinavian apron** (page 101, right) is made in a soft cotton fabric (22 inches of 36 inch fabric is required).

A bias trimming the same colour as the cotton is folded double and sewn to the sides and bottom

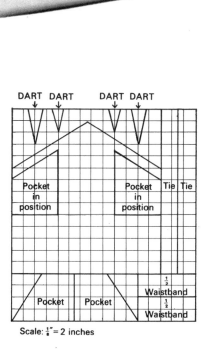

of the apron, and then a lace edging is added. Gather the apron top into a waistband of the cotton 3 inches broad and 17 inches long, adding ties that are the same breadth and 30 inches long.

To make the hanging pocket, cut two circles of the fabric $7\frac{3}{4}$ inches in diameter. Decorate one circle with trimmings and rickrack and then line each circle of fabric. Stitch the circles together around the bottom and sides, and edge with lace the same as that edging the apron itself. Attach the pocket to the apron, with two lengths of the fabric $2 \times 8\frac{1}{2}$ inches in size; each is folded wrong side uppermost, the outer edges are sewn together and the pieces turned right side out. One end is sewn to each side of the pocket and the other ends to each side of the waistband as shown.

GOTLAND · SWEDEN

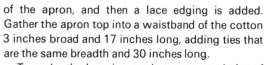

DART	DART		DART	DART		
Pocket in position			Pocket in position		Tie	Tie
						$\frac{1}{2}$ Waistband
Pocket		Pocket				$\frac{1}{2}$ Waistband

Scale: $\frac{1}{4}$" = 2 inches

Floral Banded Apron

Any colour combination you wish of cotton and embroidered tape would be effective for the floral banded apron. The fabric is a piece of satin-finished, ribbed cotton, 34 inches wide and $17\frac{1}{2}$ inches long.

Make narrow hems on the sides of the fabric and face the lower edge with woven flowered ribbon using toning or contrasting colours. For the pockets two pieces of fabric 7 inches square are turned under $\frac{1}{4}$ inch on three sides, and the top of the pocket faced with ribbon and hemmed in position about $4\frac{1}{4}$ inches from the top.

The top edge of the apron is gathered to 18 inches, and a piece of the woven ribbon 2 yards long is top-stitched to wide bias tape back-to-back, with 18 inches left free at the centre, the lower edge here being left open. Mark the centre of this 18 inches with a pin and also mark the gathered apron top in the centre.

Place centre to centre, with the apron top between the woven ribbon and bias tape, spread the gathers evenly, tack through the three layers of material and top-stitch to form the waistband and ties.

A smaller version for a child could be made more appealing, perhaps, with animal or nursery rhyme motifs on the woven ribbon or braid.

Rickrack Apron

A self-coloured apron such as the pink one (page 103, left) can be trimmed with coloured rickrack forming a design.

The basic apron is cut out from a soft cotton or cotton-mixture fabric in a flared style. To achieve the fullness cut three-quarters of a circle from the fabric. This forms the apron shape. Hem the sides and bottom and then make the waistband and ties. The ties are $3\frac{1}{4}$ inches wide and so are gathered into the narrower 2 inch wide waistband and stitched. Rickrack can also be used to decorate the ties.

Finally stitch or machine the ties and waistband to the apron.

For the design shown here wide wavy rickrack is machine-stitched across the waistband and then in two well-spaced rows down the sides and along the bottom. A row of narrow rickrack is then centred between these two rows to add contrast, and stitched in place.

Differently shaped trimmings which follow the curve of the apron are a simple but effective addition to a plain style. For example, the rickrack may be stitched on to form a series of loops, or a child's name in cursive script. Trace the name on to the material before attempting to stitch on the braid.

Gardening Apron

This useful gardening apron is made of $1\frac{1}{4}$ yards of 40 inch wide heavy cotton.

The measurements for the apron (here 15 inches wide at the waist and 19 inches at the hips) can be varied to suit the wearer. For extra strength the apron can be cut out twice and both shapes sewn together. The apron is slit 13 inches up from the hemline to form legs and the edges are bound with the same bias tape as is used for the other edges and the waist. Patches are cut out from iron-on material of different colours, placed on the apron at knee level, and backed with pieces of foam rubber to act as padding during any kneeling operations.

Pockets are a must on this sort of apron; these measure $9\frac{1}{2}$ inches × $7\frac{1}{2}$ inches, and can be made even bigger. A very useful addition is made to one of the pockets if it is divided down its length, that is, on the $9\frac{1}{2}$ inch measurement, making two divisions which are handy for smaller gardening implements such as secateurs, which are otherwise apt to get left on a bush or garden wall.

Ties $2\frac{3}{4}$ inches wide and $20\frac{1}{4}$ inches long are hemmed and stitched to the waist, and narrow ties added to secure the legs.

P.V.C. would also be a suitable material for this practical apron.

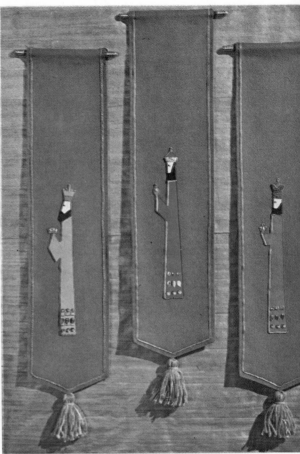

Christmas Design and Ideas

This section includes ideas and instructions for a variety of wall hangings, Christmas cards and tree decorations that will be fun to make. They look attractive and will give the added satisfaction of being something you have created for yourself.

There will be no difficulty in obtaining any of the materials or equipment necessary for the five ideas illustrated on these two pages. Gesso is the only unusual material, made by adding glue size to the plaster of Paris to slow down the drying process, in order to allow all the detail to be added to the three very elaborate kings and their gifts. The glue size prevents the plaster of Paris from cracking so easily and also helps to harden it.

A sharp knife, such as a Stanley knife, will be needed to cut the lino, otherwise a pair of scissors is the only cutting tool necessary. A small pair of tweezers will help with the arranging of the seeds on the very decorative seed panel.

A little patience, time and ingenuity is all that is needed to create these ideas successfully.

The Three Kings provide the subject for the **seed mosaic** (above left). The backing is plywood which is spread with glue. Into a light coloured background of rice or barley are set seeds in different colours from the vast selection available; greenish yellow broad beans, green dried peas, dark coffee beans and smaller seeds such as oats, lentils, pearl barley, and black cloves or, from the garden, any coloured seeds ranging from poppy seeds to honesty pods and sycamore wings. Arrange these to form pleasing shapes and colours for the Kings in their flowing robes. Surface

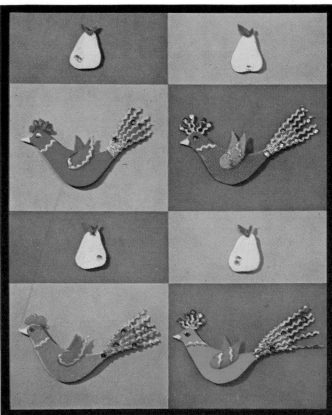

protection for the mosaic is provided by acrylic lacquer. For further details of the technique see Seed Mosaics, page 76.

The Three Kings are also the theme of the **wall hangings** (above right). A felt background is lined with suede cloth. Elongated figures cut out of felt are hand-sewn to the background and trimmed with sequins. Gold braid and tassels finish off the hangings which are suspended from curtain rods.

The mosaic (page 105, top left) is done on plywood panels 2 × 5 feet in size. First of all outline the Three Kings on linoleum; cut the shapes out and glue them on the wooden background. Then cover the linoleum with gesso. This is made by adding water to plaster of Paris to make a thin creamy liquid. Allow to stand, then pour off surplus water. Mix four parts of water to 1 part of glue size and add to plaster of Paris.

Into the gesso press the bits and pieces which you have collected to make up the Kings and their garments. Braids, sequins, beads, pearls, glass, gold and silver, plastic material and scraps of coloured fabric are some ideas for adding texture to the clothing as a contrast to the smooth plywood background.

For this wall design inspired by the carol, 'The Twelve Days of Christmas', partridges are set with golden pears on a background of coloured felt rectangles. Gold rickrack makes the tail and head feathers, and the eyes are sequins. The designs are glued to the background which is framed with firm black ribbon or seam binding.

Cut paper into
triangle, mark
lines, crease,
and staple.

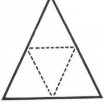

Versatile Christmas Triangles

Two sizes of these Christmas decorations can be made from equilateral paper triangles (8 inches and 12 inches in size). Spray one side of the triangle cut from coloured paper with gold paint, and use the other side as the outside. Fold the triangles along the dotted line as shown above, with points overlapping $\frac{3}{4}$ inch or 1 inch. Use staples to hold the points together. Ornaments (page 107) take four such triangles, stapled together as shown and attached to a square backing. Use this idea as a basis for other such decorations; join up two triangle shapes (glue the two flat sides together) and hang them by one corner.

The blue, green and gold tree (above) was planned with ten of these decorations as its upright.

To make the stars two concentric circles are drawn, one slightly larger than the finished star, and one to give the length of each point. Cut out the larger circle and fold into sixteen sections. Unfold and draw the star by joining each alternate intersection of a fold with the inner circle. Cut the star shape out, and fold the centre line on each point up and the alternate lines down.

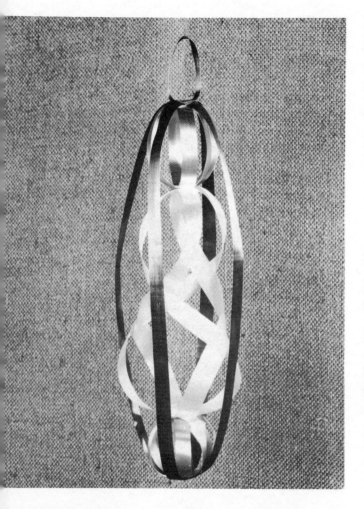

Ribbon Designs

Satin ribbon decorations to be hung on trees or to decorate Christmas gifts can be made in intricate or simple designs of all colours. Here are some ideas using plain and fancy ribbon to start you off.

For example, the long ornament (above left) has a spiral centre made by twisting large loops of ribbon and stitching them together so that they hang in a spiral shape. Then add a ball of ribbon loops to each end. Several long loops hold the three shapes together.

The round shape (top right) is made by surrounding a central circle of ribbon with a longer piece in a contrasting colour, looped and fastened at regular intervals round the circumference. The spaces between the loops are decorated with cut-out gold or silver stars.

A selection of other ornaments can be made in any size using the illustrations as a guide.

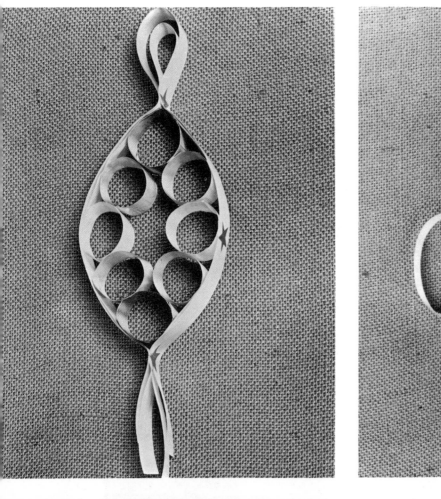

Christmas Tree Decorations

These two attractive tree decorations achieve their unusual effect with the use of ordinary pillow ticking

The simple shape on the left was made by cutting a pattern first of all by drawing one half of the shape, folding on a centre line and cutting through the folded paper following the drawn line. This process ensures that both sides are exactly the same.

The pattern is placed on a piece of thin cardboard and outlined with pencil or a tracing wheel and then cut out. The pattern is then pinned to the ticking, making sure the woven lines are straight from left to right before cutting out. To give a Christmas-like touch, a wide band of green ribbon with a narrow band of red ribbon superimposed on it, are sewn across the centre and three flower

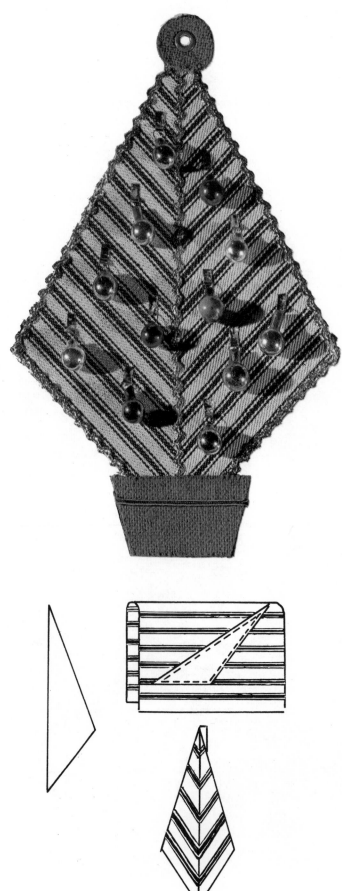

shapes, cut from a narrow lace, are each attached by a French knot through the centre of a sequin. The ticking and its decoration are then stuck to the card to make it firmer. A hole is then pierced in the top and an eyelet inserted, and a scarlet collar of ribbon added to the neck of the shape. Cord or ribbon can, of course, be threaded through the eyelet to attach the decoration to the tree, the back being covered with gold or silver paper.

The highly conventional tree shape on page 110, top right, is really rather tricky to make, but cleverly designed: the ticking suggests the branches of a tree and the little baubles suggest the fruits hanging from them. To make the pattern, one side of the tree in the illustration is traced or enlarged and cut out. The cutting out of the material is very carefully planned so that the 'branches' on both sides of the tree are at the same angle to the trunk and so that both sides of the tree are on the right side of the material.

The material is folded with stripes matching and running horizontally. The pattern is placed with the short side of the triangular pattern along a stripe, pinned in position and cut out. With right sides together, the longest sides of the triangle are sewn together, the shape opened out and the seam pressed open on the wrong side. This operation is repeated and gold gimp added to both shapes on the centre seam, either by hand or by machine, to make a trunk. The outline of the tree is also emphasized with gold gimp and little Christmas baubles added to the branches with loops of narrow gold ribbon.

The tub to hold the tree is made either by tracing again, or enlarging the illustration and cutting the shape twice in three-ply wood. These pieces of wood are stuck together, with the base of the tree between them, and then covered with green hessian and decorated with a stripe of green gimp.

As an alternative to the baubles, gold or silver embroidery in the spaces between the stripes make an attractive feature. Highly decorative stitches, such as Portuguese knotted stem stitch, raised chain band, Spanish knotted feather stitch or zigzag chain stitch could all be used with varying kinds and weights of thread to make them even more interesting. A good dictionary of stitches is a very good investment allowing various experiments to be made and favourite stitches discovered.

Crêpe Paper Flowers

This tree arrangement of blue and green flowers is made from crêpe paper. Cut a strip of crêpe paper and hand stitch or machine stitch (with a long stitch) one side of it, leaving the thread ends loose. The other long edge of the strip is cut into a fringe three quarters of the width of the strip.

Do the same with several green and blue strips of crêpe paper and then gather the stitched edge of each so that you have several circles of fringed crêpe paper to make your flower. The centre is formed by half a plastic ball covered with crepe paper.

The various sizes of flowers (3 to 8 inches in diameter) are attached first to wire covered with green chenille and then to a curtain rod to form the outline and branches of a tree. A frame of any shape can be added to display the flowers.

Try out this design also in the conventional Christmassy colours of red, white and green, or with accents of gold in the centres of the flowers.

Christmas Mobiles

Christmas Mobiles

The hanging decorations shown on page 112 can be used year after year. The basic shapes are cut from heavy cardboard covered in hessian. This is cut to the same shape, leaving a 1 inch border to allow for folding over the edge of the cardboard. Also clip or notch the edges of the cut-out hessian to allow for a smooth fit on curves and corners. The hessian is glued to the front of the cardboard shape and the allowance is folded over and glued to the back. Cover the raw edges with adhesive tape, or back them with gold or silver paper.

Fabric loops attached to curtain rings are glued or sewn on to the hessian for hanging the ornaments from ribbons. They can be backed with hessian, or two ornaments of the same shape can be used back to back (in this case, they should be blind-stitched together along the side seams).

Various materials can be used to decorate the front; gold and silver paper, sequins, rickrack and gimp are some suggestions shown.

Christmas Labels

Gift cards or present labels are easy to make and offer considerable scope for ingenuity. As a basis, cut coloured paper into squares or triangles. Fold them if you wish to decorate only the outside, or else use one side for the greeting and the other for your design, which may be a cut-out in contrasting colour (as shown below) or textured decoration with gold dust, sequins or beads.

For these, it is easier to draw your design lightly on the paper first in pencil, trace the lines with a fine brush dipped in glue and then scatter your chosen bits and pieces on the glue. All sorts of different colours and textures can make up animal shapes (with little pieces of coloured felt for noses or ears and bright sequins for eyes), sunbursts (in bright yellows and oranges) or for children a copy of their favourite toy or story character.

For silhouette name cards (right, and pages 114, 115) write names in flowing letters along fold line of a piece of folded paper. Cut out carefully and paste on to card.

A thin card is more suitable than cartridge paper for this kind of decoration as it must stay crisp and attractive. As quite a few are usually needed it could be a good idea to make a stencil and so save a lot of time. First decide on the kind of design. It could be geometric, abstract or naturalistic in character or be a name (as shown), or word such as 'Greetings'.

If the design is to be symmetrical draw a centre line on a piece of heavy cartridge paper. Draw one half of the design on one side of the centre line and take a tracing with a soft pencil. Reverse the tracing to the other side of the centre line and, matching all shapes and lines, press the design through to the heavy cartridge paper with the sharp point of a hard pencil.

All the shapes must be carefully considered to avoid cutting away too much background, leaving the stencil too fragile. A very sharp knife is necessary and a piece of glass on which to cut. Printers' inks and a stencil brush are needed for the actual printing.

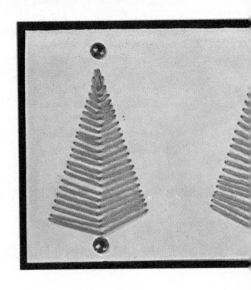

Christmas Cards

It can be fun to make your own Christmas cards, especially for children. Here are some ideas (pages 114-17) you might like to try out and perhaps elaborate.

First make a good choice of suitable paper. Whatman hot or cold pressed is a rather expensive paper to buy and it is normally used for water-colour painting. It is possible to buy it in various thicknesses or 'weights'. The hot pressed has a smooth texture and the cold pressed a rough, more interesting surface. Both are possible to use as backgrounds or as cut-outs. Cartridge paper is not so expensive to use and it also comes in various weights, but is not available in colour.

Sugar paper, however, is another rough sur-faced paper which is available in a few colours and is very attractive as a background.

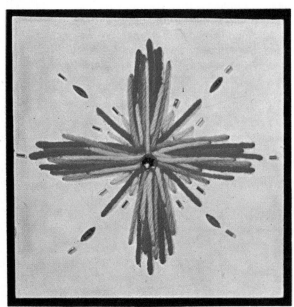

Japanese paper is quite expensive, but there is an imitation on the market which is very attractive. Plain newsprint or lining paper are both very good and cheap for experiments or children's efforts. Cambridge paper, Oxford paper, Manilla and frieze paper are all medium weight and available in a wide colour range.

Fluorescent poster paper, obtainable in vivid vibrating colours, radiant metallic papers in gold, silver, green, red and blue and fancy papers in a range of gay festive patterns are some of the more exotic materials to choose from. Texturewise, felt, leatherette, and suede papers can be very interesting, as is Fablon which, of course, is self-adhesive and therefore very clean to use. Some of the gummed nursery papers are very easy to handle and can be bought already cut into star and moon shapes.

Vellum is, perhaps, the most expensive paper, which as a kind of compensation seems to have a Christmassy feeling all its own. In contrast, tissue paper is, perhaps, one of the cheapest, and it again has a dainty quality peculiar to itself.

If none of these papers are firm enough it may be

necessary to use card, and here again there is quite a large choice. Cardboard is obtainable in white and colours as well as in various thicknesses. Bristol board, Inveresk and Essex board are three names to look for and also mounting board of various weights. A considerable number of satisfactory glues are on the market for fixing on decorative details. Uhu, Evostik, Bostik, Gripfix, Gloy, Resin W and Araldite are expensive but worth using.

The card with the **stylized star** (page 114, top left) is made from stiff coloured paper. Fold the sheet in half and fold the top half back in half again. Cut out two slightly differently shaped stars, the pale pink one in stiff paper, the red one in tissue paper, and add a fancy gold paper star on top. Glue is used to attach the stars to the card and to each other with centre points on the front fold. Try out various colours and designs until you find what you want.

Three examples show the use of **cut-outs** of different textures on plain coloured paper; scallop decoration in the same paper as the cut-out has been used at the foot of page 114, a tinted background and gold dust add interest to the card (top right page 114), while top left page 115 combines sequins made into flowers and a ribbon bow with the cut-out.

Children's sewing cards provide the inspiration for the **woollen star card** (top right, page 115) and the three **shaded Christmas trees** (foot of pages 114 and 115). Sketch your design on coloured or white cardboard, punch holes to outline the design and for shadings inside this outline. Lace wool of different colours through the holes and secure them at the back. Sequins, shiny discs or lettering can be added to complete the cards.

The **standing Christmas trees card** (page 115 foot) is a simple idea. Stiff white paper is folded in half and slits made across the fold so that strips about half an inch wide can be pushed out. These stand up, and after the paper has been glued to another piece of stiff green paper to form the background, blue and green triangles are glued to the front of these partially cut out strips. Both triangles and base can be decorated.

The pleasing colour combinations of the card (below left) set off the idea of a **Christmas bell**. Again, standard size stiff white paper is folded in half, then folded twice on each half 1¾ and 3½ inch from the ends. Make the bell by drawing and then cutting out half a bell shape, not quite to the rim (as the diagram shows) on each side of the centre fold.

The white paper is glued to a red stiff paper backing and the decorative red bell cut-out is made from tissue paper and glued on to the white bell.

The **white pleated tree** (page 115, top) has tiers of white paper folded in accordion pleats and glued into the fold of a sheet of stiff green paper folded in half. A yellow base and embossed gold star finish off the card. This is a basic design which you can use with a variety of dark backgrounds and finishing touches.

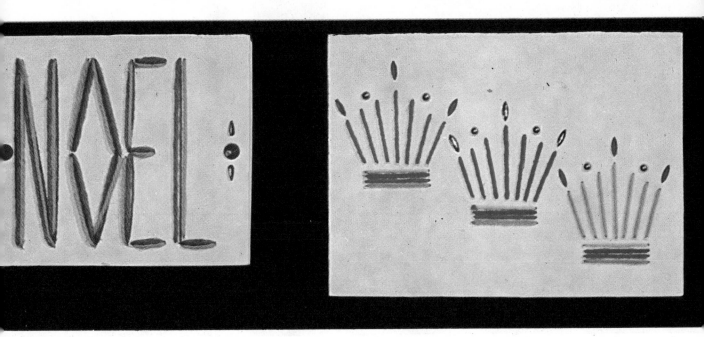

Gift Decorations

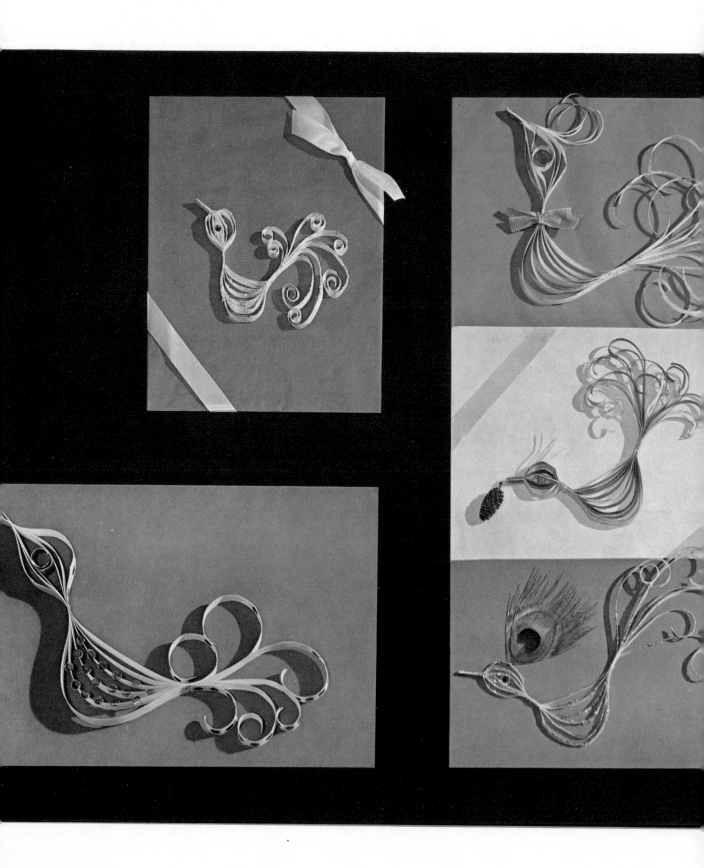

Birds made from paper strips are a way of decorating gifts inexpensively (page 118).

The basic design is simple. Seven or more strips of paper 12 inches in length by $\frac{1}{2}$, $\frac{1}{4}$ or $\frac{1}{8}$ inches in breadth (depending on the weight of paper you are using) cut from shelf or typing paper (or any paper which will curl when pulled over the blade of a pair of scissors or twisted round a pencil) are laid with the ends together and stapled at one end to form the bill. The head is then formed by adjusting and varying the length of strips until they are circular in shape; secure them with a staple to form the neck. Adjust the strips similarly to make the body shape and staple at the beginning of the tail. The latter is formed by curling the strips round a pencil or pulling them over the blade of a pair of scissors. Shorten some strands to make the tail uneven.

To add a crest to the top of the head either split one or more of the strips of paper before the neck staple is put in and curl them up or add feathers or fabric to the head. A middle strip can be split at the same time to form an eye.

Finally add touches of paint here and there. Sequins, feathers, ribbon, circles of coloured or metallic paper can be glued on. Or, alternatively, brush parts of the bird with gold or silver paint. Buttons, seeds, small shells and circles of coloured trimming are a few of the individual touches you can add.

Gift Wrappings

Wrapping Christmas gifts can be fascinating. These are some ideas that you might like to try out.

They make use of differently coloured and textured ribbons but other materials at hand can equally enhance the intriguing look of gifts.

For boxes in a single colour wrap several ribbon widths in a toning colour around the lid and tape or glue them to the underside (with the ribbon covering the sides of the box lid too), allowing some of the colour to show through on top. For example, black ribbon can be used to cover a gold box.

By basket weaving strips of ribbon an unusual effect is created. Tape equal lengths of ribbon (long enough to be taped to the underside) across the box top. The strands from the two sides are woven neatly into these. On larger boxes or ones with attractively coloured lids, spaces can be left between the ribbons to allow colour to show through. Or, to make use of a fancy box with a shop imprint, simply cover the imprint with a strand of broad ribbon, then tape lengths of narrower matching or toning ribbons on each side of this and add a bow to finish off the lid.

Advent Wall Hangings

These colourful felt hangings loop over brass curtain rods. Decorations include felt figures and numbers, braid, small toys and wrapped sweets.

The designs are traced on to the back of the felt, cut out and then reversed ready for sewing on the figures. The figures are stuffed before they are sewn

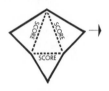

on. Hands are made of double pieces of felt, sewn together then stuffed and tacked in position. Tuck back the edge of the sleeve so that the hand appears to emerge from it.

Two sturdy elves copied from a German elf doll stand guard over a Christmas tree, while sweets tied with ribbon bows mark the days from December 1st to Christmas Day.

The Dutch boy and girl hanging uses the same basic design. Bright yellow wool should be used for her pigtails. Ten little elves run over a wool embroidered hill on their way to the candle-decorated Christmas tree. The upright style has a tubby white felt snowman well stuffed with cotton wool.

All the pictures use oddments of bright wool, sequins, glittering braid and tinsel and the method of embroidery used is really a form of quilting.

Pyramid Tree Baubles

To copy these attractive Christmas tree decorations first enlarge the diagram (page 120, right). Make quite sure all six sides of the triangles are the same length and that all three base measurements are the same.

Place the pattern on a piece of firm cardboard, mark round it carefully with a pencil and cut it out. Firmly score the outline of the inner triangle by using a bone folder against a metal rule.

Choose a material with an interesting texture that is light enough to make neat seams along the edges of the finished pyramids. Place the pattern on the selected material making sure that the base of the centre triangle matches the weft of the material. Allow $\frac{1}{4}$ inch turnings all the way round and cut out. Cut the pattern shape into the three triangles and abandon the base shape. Lay the pattern pieces in place on the material, pin carefully and tack the outline of the inner triangle.

Decide on the materials and design of the decorations and arrange them on an imaginary centre line drawn from the tip of each triangle to the centre of each base. Add a small bead in the centre of each sequin to fix it securely. Add the gimp at the base when the shape has been assembled.

Place the decorated material wrong side uppermost on the table and arrange the cardboard shape in position on it. Stick the material turning allowance down on to the card all round and fold up into shape. Slip-stitch the sides of the three triangles in pairs with invisible slip-stitching completing the decorated pyramid. Add a loop at the top for hanging on the Christmas tree.

Glittering Stars

The only material required to make these bright decorations is a number of tins. These can be cut and twisted into a variety of different shapes, but remember to wear strong gloves of cloth or leather to protect your hands from cuts.

Use tins of various sizes, with gold and silver interiors. Shears or strong scissors will cut the tins and they are easy to twist into shapes with pliers.

The first step is to strip off the outside paper and erase any printing with nail varnish remover. Take off the top rim and cut the sides down to the base in strips of varied widths according to the design. After cutting the strips, spread them flat and then use pliers to twist and curl them into shapes. The examples shown on page 123 are the basic shapes. The strips can be curved into spiral shapes and the ends curled with pliers, or they can be arched into triangular shapes and doubled back towards the

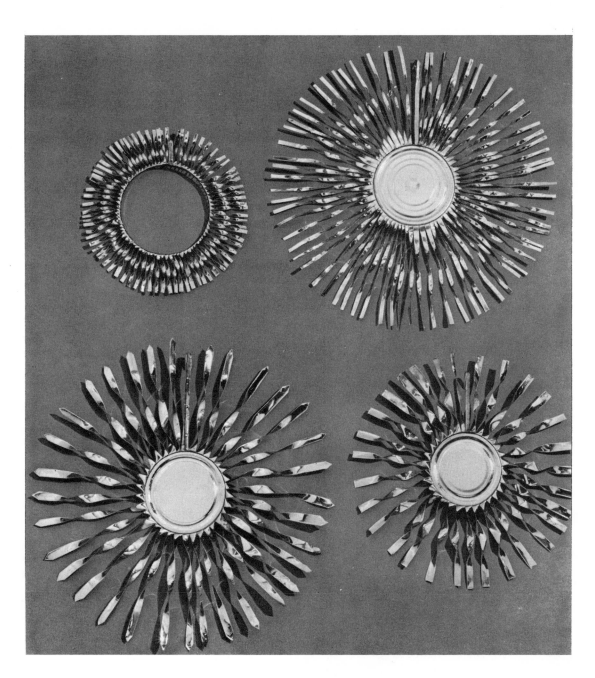

centre of the tin. Try other ideas; layers of circles with the strips shaped into petals make a flower, or cut leaf shapes and animal shapes with crimped or curled edges.

For smaller shapes, cut the lids of tins into strips in the same way as the whole tins. For example, cut a lid evenly, almost to the centre, in sixteen strips. The centre left uncut measures less than the size of a sixpence.

For variety, some stars are sprayed with white paint topped with gold spray and glitter, or a tassel made from colourful lurex wool is tied through a hole in the centre of the lid (made with a bradawl) and knotted at the back.

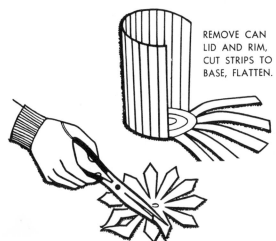

REMOVE CAN LID AND RIM, CUT STRIPS TO BASE, FLATTEN.

Christmas Wall Hangings

These contrasting Christmas wall hangings are simple and colourful. You can make them all with felt and a selection of trimmings using these pictures as a basic guide.

The colourful **partridges** wall hanging (below) has turquoise and chartreuse felt birds on a deep purple felt background measuring 13½ × 18 inches.

A symmetrical design has been chosen for this panel and so the placing of the two birds must be given careful consideration.

First cut a piece of tracing paper the exact size the finished panel is to be and fold it in half along its longer side making a sharp crease, forming a rectangle 9 inches on its base and 13½ inches on its side.

Make a pattern from a suitable photograph or drawing for the right hand bird. Slip the pattern between the folded tracing paper and place the bird nicely with its head facing the crease, and with the crease on the left. Trace the outline carefully but ignore the details of wings, tail and head. Add the lines representing the branches of the tree and remove the pattern shape. Turn the tracing over so that the crease is now on the right and re-trace the drawing with the bird now facing in the opposite direction. Open the tracing paper out flat and the birds will be facing each other in exactly the right position on the tracing. Place a sheet of waxed carbon paper face down on the felt background and place the tracing over it, then with a very sharp hard pencil press the design on to the felt by re-drawing the design with a firm line.

When the birds are cut out and assembled there will be no doubt as to where they are to be placed on the panel.

The heads, wings and tails can be cut from one colour of felt and the bodies from another. As each shape is cut out, place it in position under the tracing, with waxed carbon paper between and draw in the detail. Glue trimmings and rickrack in position on the finished bird before attaching to the background. Sequins are used for eyes, rickrack for detail on the birds' wings and tails, gold soutache braid is used for the branches on which the birds are perched, and 2½ yards of gold fringe forms the border. At the top of the hanging the felt is folded behind the fringe and stitched over a dowel from which it hangs.

The **Three Kings** hanging (page 125 left) uses a simple technique but achieves a very dramatic effect. The centre line is marked faintly from top to bottom with tailors' chalk and the top of each head and the middle of the hem of each skirt is also marked to ensure that the figures are placed directly beneath each other on the panel, each occupying ⅓ of its height. The same basic patterns are used for the robes, sleeves and gift boxes. The sleeves could be either brocade, satin or lamé. The robes are felt, a narrow gold cord outlines the face, rich braid makes the trimmings and gifts and the distinctive shapes for the crowns.

A fast drying glue is used to stick the details to the shapes, making sure the minimum amount is used so that it does not soak through to show on the right side. The figures are then centred on the line already marked in the background with tops of heads and hemlines matching the guide lines already made. The surplus tailors' chalk is dusted off and the panel mounted on plywood with an edging of braid showing all round.

The **Christmas Tree** (page 125 left) hanging is 12 × 36 inches in size, held by a 13 inch wood dowel painted gold. Green (1½ yards) and sapphire (1¼ yards) rickrack, red (2½ yards) and gold (5½ yards) rickrack, gold braid (1¼ yards) and gold fringe (1 yard) form the shapes of the trees. Fill in the trees with other decorative braids and frame the hanging with gold braid.

The easiest way to do this design is to sketch the tree outlines on felt and use glue to attach the trimmings.

If you have time to spare a more satisfactory method would be to couch the rickrack and braid into position with an invisible thread and hem the top edge of the braid to secure it in position. By this means that odd spot of glue in just the wrong position is avoided. Various colours and weights of thread and elaborate stitches would again replace the braids and rickrack as has already been suggested on page 100.

The **Concentric Circles** wall design uses the same techniques. The felt background (18½ × 27

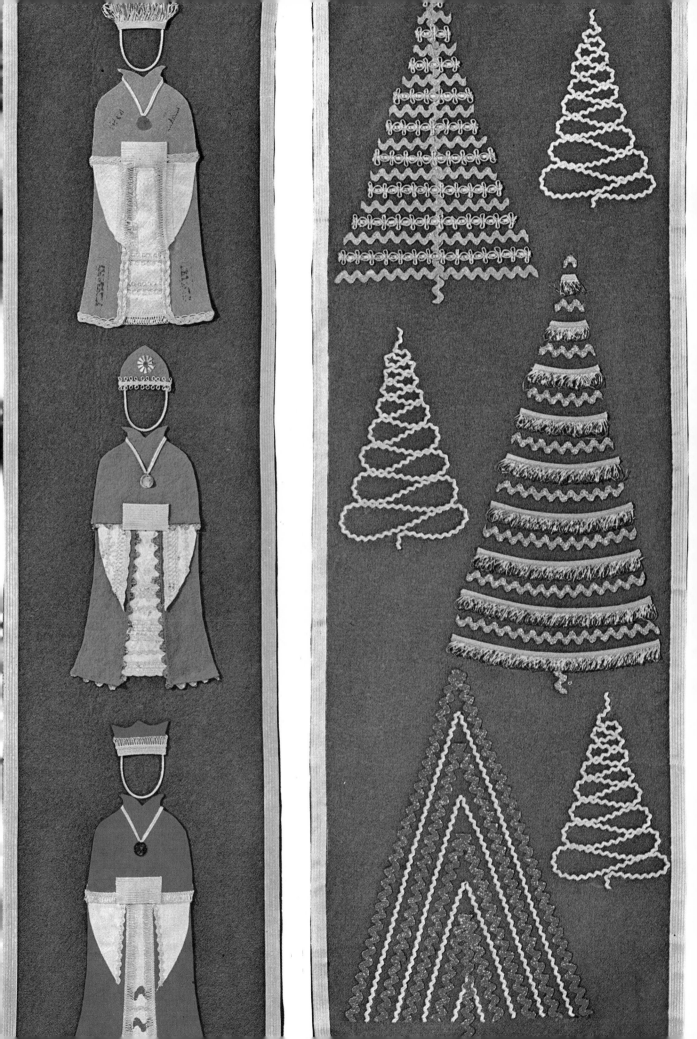

inches) is looped over a wood dowel and glued. The frame is gold braid. Draw circles on the felt by tying string to a pencil, holding the end of the string and drawing a circle with the pencil.

A more reliable method would be to use a compass. If the line is going to be concealed a biro or felt pen might make a more satisfactory line than a pencil in the compass.

Circles of different diameters are drawn inside one another and the circles spaced out on the felt. The centre motif, a scarlet foil star, is backed by a gold star and gold ornaments added. Sequins are used for the centres of the smaller circles and three widths of gold metallic braid, orange and sapphire

rickrack and gold fringing ($\frac{1}{4}$, $\frac{1}{2}$ and $\frac{3}{4}$ inches wide).

This basically geometric arrangment needs very careful planning. The centre of the panel can be found by folding the felt background in half lengthwise and then in half again widthwise. A more accurate method would be to make a plan on a piece of paper the exact size the design is to be; as this is less bulky than the felt, the folding will be more accurate and the centre more easily found. The centres of the smaller circles could be found by bisecting the right angles in the four corners and marking the centres of each the same distance in from the corners on the bisection line.